From
Fear
to
Eternity

ALSO BY ROBERT ROSENTHAL

From Never-Mind to Ever-Mind

From Loving One to One Love

From
Fear
to
Eternity

The Journey of
A Course in Miracles

ROBERT ROSENTHAL, M.D.

MEDIA

Published by Gildan Media LLC
aka G&D Media.
www.GandDmedia.com

FIRST EDITION: 2022

Front cover design by David Rheinhardt of Pyrographx

Interior design by Meghan Day Healey of Story Horse, LLC.

Library of Congress Cataloging-in-Publication Data is available upon request

ISBN: 978-1-7225-1022-0

10   9   8   7   6   5   4   3   2   1

Contents

Foreword. 1
Preface 3

1 The Journey. 9
2 Freedom. 21
3 The Body. 57
4 The Separation 99
5 The World 111
6 The Real World 127
7 Decision. 141

Notes. 153
Endnotes. 155

Foreword

This book is an exploration of *A Course in Miracles*, a self-help study course in mind healing that was first published in 1975. It has since sold approximately 3 million copies and touched the lives of countless people worldwide.

The Course is a channeled text, meaning that the individual who wrote it down, Helen Schucman, did not consider herself as the author. Rather, she said, she was taking dictation from a "Voice" that identified itself as Jesus Christ. Her associate Bill Thetford helped her in the transcription and editing.

This book is the third in a series by Robert Rosenthal, MD, copresident of the Foundation for Inner Peace, the Course's publisher. It follows on his first two works: *From Never-Mind to Ever-Mind: Transforming the Self to Embrace Miracles* (2019) and *From Loving One to One Love: Transforming Relationships through "A Course in Miracles"* (2020).

Both of these have been published by Gildan Media. Readers wanting more on the background of the Course are referred to these two books.

Preface

by Robert Rosenthal, MD

A *Course in Miracles* takes us on a journey. It is not an outer journey. Our bodies do not travel somewhere new. It is a journey within, in which our mind learns to shift from a false sense of who and what we are to reawaken to our true identity as spirit. This can never change, no matter what we do, no matter how much we may try to close our eyes and shut out the truth. It can never change, because it is beyond our ability to change: it was created by God.

In practical terms, the journey of *A Course in Miracles* can be summarized as leading us "from fear to eternity." Granted, it's an amusing bit of wordplay based on the title of the famous 1953 Hollywood movie *From Here to Eternity*. But it is apt. We begin in fear and at the journey's end realize we are in eternity, and always have been.

According to *A Course in Miracles*, we are born into a world of separation. We believe that we are unique, individual beings. We inhabit physical bodies that live, interact, and move about within a world that is for the most part beyond our ability to control. "Shit happens." That includes unexpected illness, accidents, floods, tornadoes, pandemics, financial crashes, terrorist attacks, wars, and so on. Ultimately, this individual self must die. It is tied to the body, and the body is not immortal. The fact that we don't know which day will be our last provokes a great deal of fear. Everything we know, everyone we love—it could all come crashing into oblivion at any moment. Fear is the natural state of the ego. It is *our* natural state if we choose to identify with the ego and reject spirit.

Of course, we do our best not to think about the inevitability of death. We paper over life's uncertainties with attempts at control. We take steps to stay healthy, protect our bodies from damage, and extend their lives as long as possible.

The predictability of routine can also be very reassuring. Getting out of bed each morning, showering, sipping coffee, doing whatever we do throughout the day, then returning home to dinner, leisure time, bed—these convey an illusion of predictability and safety. The sun will rise again in the morning. Christmas and your birthday will cycle back around for another year. This veneer of predictability is comforting and probably necessary. Who could make it through the day if they constantly ruminated about impending death, much less the demise of all humankind? Physics tells us that the universe itself will one day come to a halt. It's only a matter of time.

Time is not infinite. It strings out in increments of hours, weeks, years, all of which seem to slip by faster the older we get. Remember how when you were a child, summers seemed almost endless? July stretched on for ages, followed by an equally generous August. Not so anymore. Twenty years is a lifetime when you turn twenty-one; at sixty it's merely one-third.

What has an end is fearful; what is unknown and beyond our control is quietly terrifying. This seems to be our lot, and we make the best of it. Yet we cannot ignore those glimmers of something more, something greater—moments that sail free of the linear press of time—moments the English poet William Wordsworth called "intimations of immortality." In such moments (which I called "perfect moments" in my book *From Never-Mind to Ever-Mind*) we are granted a taste the infinite and discover there the antidote to our fears. The cure for time's relentless death march turns out to be timelessness. Once experienced, the desire to recapture these moments, to make them endure somehow and become our permanent state, becomes the goal of life's journey. It is also the goal of *A Course in Miracles*.

There can be no remedy for fear within the ego's narrow concept of self and world. Fear is inherent—the default setting. Therefore, to move past fear we must learn another way of understanding the self and the world, one that has no relation to the limited ego mind. We must learn to embrace eternity.

*   *   *

There is only one lesson in the Course's Workbook for Students that's repeated over and over (twenty-six times in all). It is this: "*I am as God created me*" or "*I am still as God cre-*

ated me."[1] We are told that this simple statement on its own would be sufficient to awaken us from our dream of separation and suffering—if we fully believed it. Obviously, we do not. But all our searching will be futile if we start out from a false premise about who or what is doing the searching.

If our true identity is the Son of God, as the Course tells us, and if that identity is shared by all minds, then we will not find it in illusions of separation. If the goal of the journey is remembering God, then nothing else will do. "*It is impossible to remember God in secret and alone. . . . The lonely journey fails because it has excluded what it would find.*"[2]

The journey back to God and our true Self—the journey from fear to eternity—is the only journey worth taking because it is the only one with a real purpose. The purpose always determines the direction of the journey: where it begins, how it proceeds, and how it ends. The Course points out that without a purpose, your journey will be rudderless. Without a clear endpoint, you can never reach your destination. We only know the journey is completed if it has a clear purpose and that purpose has been accomplished.

What can I seek for, Father, but Your Love? Perhaps I think I seek for something else, a something I have called by many names. Yet is Your Love the only thing I seek, or ever sought. For there is nothing else that I could ever really want to find. Let me remember You. What else could I desire but the truth about myself?[3]

I was created as the thing I seek. I am the goal the world is searching for. I am God's Son, His one eternal Love.[4]

In the pages that follow, we will look at various aspects of the Course's teaching that lead us past the obstacles to peace and open the way to the final goal: God.

1

The Journey

The journey to God is merely the reawakening of the knowledge of where you are always, and what you are forever. It is a journey without distance to a goal that has never changed.[1]

The journey is not long except in dreams.[2]

When I was younger, I loved to travel. At the age of sixteen, I backpacked through Europe and Scandinavia with a friend on a rail pass; at twenty-five, I embarked on a trip around the world, only to break my leg hiking the South Island of New Zealand, which forced me to return home. I have driven across the United States multiple times on different routes: Interstate 80 through the Midwest and Rockies; Interstates 30 and 10 through the endless expanse of Texas and the Southwest; and I-90 through Minnesota, North Dakota, and Montana. I've been stopped by less than friendly cops and by glowering thunderstorms that shed rain so furious that the windshield wipers couldn't keep up.

What was it I sought on these excursions? Adventure, that's for sure—so long as it never veered into real danger. A sense of freedom from the daily routine; days where my only concern upon awakening was how many miles to cover and where to overnight. And of course the encounter with new people and different cultures, like the elderly Swiss couple I passed as they strolled down an Alpine path. They responded to my exhausted query, "How much further to the top?" by quipping that the answer depended on where I was from.

I also enjoyed the cachet of having traveled to so many different places at such a young age on my own. I wanted to impress and to be impressive. Looking back, I also think I was testing myself. Could I handle navigating my way through a city like Amsterdam? Sleeping in a train compartment with strangers who didn't speak English? Being out of contact with my family for weeks at a time? (Remember, this was in the era before mobile phones and the Internet made a video call to Germany or China as easy as calling next door.) But there is a strong appeal in the notion of setting out to discover something new. It's almost a primal urge, something hardwired into the structure of our psyche.

We grow discontent with the known. We want to fling wide the door to change, flee the cloying press of the familiar, and depart for distant horizons. We are eager to discover hidden treasures—a gem of a restaurant, a secluded beach, an amazing conversation with someone we've only just met, or some far-off land where no one knows who we are and everything sings of starting life afresh. Journeys hold the promise of new beginnings.

Such is the appeal of the journey, but also its terror. As much as the notion of change calls out and thrills us, we simultaneously fear it. The moment we abandon the familiar and set out on a journey, a host of what-ifs swoop down on us, like hordes of cave bats awakened from slumber, flapping about in the dark corners of our mind. These what-ifs can be powerful and persuasive. They whisper of the perils that might befall us on the journey, suggesting that perhaps we should be sensible and give up before we've even begun. What if . . . things don't work out? What if . . . we lose our way? What if . . . we're attacked and robbed? What if . . . the journey actually kills us? It's always a possibility. What treasure could be worth dying for? Or the more mundane and likely possibilities: What if the destination turns out to be nothing like we imagined. What if . . . it's disappointing? Boring? And not all that different from home?

Let others sally forth to discover new worlds. We'll snuggle up at home with a good book and do our best to be content with the world as we know it. The moment we accept this, however, and cancel our plans, the urge to set forth on the journey rises up and beckons once again.

* * *

A high school English teacher of mine once opined that all literature falls into two categories. They are exemplified by the children's books *Winnie the Pooh* and *The Wizard of Oz.* Pooh and the lovable characters who live alongside him never journey anywhere, except perhaps for a friendly social visit and a cup of tea. No one strays outside the Hundred Acre Wood. Their dramas are interpersonal, and they play out within its boundaries. It's as if there were no outside world.

This has its charms. The Hundred Acre Wood could be any town or community anywhere in the world. You can live comfortably within its borders your whole life, should you choose. No wonder *Winnie the Pooh* has remained so popular with young children. They need above all else to be reassured that their relationships are secure. They crave a stable home base, not a journey they're totally unequipped to take.

By contrast, *The Wizard of Oz* is all about the journey. Dorothy has grown restless with rural farm life. Her aunt and uncle are caring but ineffectual. They make no effort to help save her dog, Toto, from being abducted and put to sleep. To save her beloved pet, Dorothy must venture far from the bounds of home. Her inner turbulence is mirrored by the twister that spins into her life, uprooting the house where she lives with her aunt and uncle and whirling it away from the familiar black-and-white wheat fields of Kansas into the marvelous, terrifying, "in living color" land of Oz.

In Oz, Dorothy is no mere orphan farm girl. She's an instant hero, for she has slain the detested Wicked Witch of the East by dropping a house on her. But Dorothy is pursued by the witch's sister, the even more terrifying Wicked Witch of the West, who seeks to avenge her sister's death and reclaim her magical ruby slippers, which Dorothy now wears. Yet Dorothy's sole wish is to return home. Accompanied by her newfound companions, the Scarecrow, Tin Man, and Cowardly Lion, she sets out on a journey—a quest to seek the counsel of the all-powerful Wizard of Oz in the expectation that he can grant her wish and return her to her Kansas home.

Just as Pooh appeals to younger children, Dorothy speaks to the older child and adolescent. They have discovered that there is an entire world beyond the family. They yearn to explore it, but also fear what may lie in wait for them. Their desire for the new rapidly succumbs to sadness over the loss of their cherished childhood home. They become homesick: not sick *of* home, as the word seems to imply, but sick *for* home.

The Wizard of Oz reveals something fundamental about the nature of the journey. We strike out into the unknown, leaving the home we know, but which no longer satisfies us, to seek a new home—a magical place where we will be welcomed, loved, and appreciated as never before. We feel we must leave home in order to find our real home. Yet as Dorothy's journey through Oz makes clear, the home we seek was never truly lost. It was with us always. The journey never occurred except in dreams. For Dorothy, it was a hallucinatory by-product of head trauma, that is, a sharp blow to the mind.

According to *A Course in Miracles,* the separation from God was just such a blow. It points out (echoing Mary Baker Eddy, founder of Christian Science) that "*the Bible says that a deep sleep fell upon Adam, and nowhere is there reference to his waking up.*"³ The Course sums up both Adam's and Dorothy's journeying in one simple, eloquent line: "*You travel but in dreams, while safe at home.*"⁴

A Course in Miracles tells us that we have no choice about setting out on a journey. However much we may avoid it, the journey is imperative. As with Dorothy, the journey will find us. "*You* will *undertake a journey because you are not at home in this world. And you* will *search for your home whether you realize where it is or not.*"⁵ The Course does sound a note of caution about the journey's goal: "*If you believe it is outside you the search will be futile, for you will be seeking it where it is not.*"⁶

We are warned against pursuing false goals and false gods, because these will never satisfy our yearning. They will keep us forever searching. Like the Hebrews of the biblical book of Exodus, forty years can pass in a heartbeat wandering the wilderness if you choose to worship golden calves. Forty years turns out to be a small price to pay if at the journey's end you finally do reach your Promised Land. But if you do not, an entire lifetime has been squandered.

*   *   *

The ego is the part of the mind that has dreamed itself separate from God. Like a poker player who refuses to fold a losing hand, it bluffs and bets the pot, confident in itself, certain of its ability to hoodwink us. The ego always tries to subvert our desire to find our way home to God in order to cement its commitment to separation. One way it achieves this is by sending us on useless journeys. Their goal is always to obtain something special for ourselves alone—

an object, a person, or an experience—something of great value that will make us unique, admirable, and desirable; something that can invest our lives with a meaning far beyond the mundane. The ego believes that such treasures can only be found outside itself. It knows its own inherent weakness and lack of value* (although it will never admit this); therefore, the last place it cares to look is within. Even when it embarks on a regimen of "self-improvement," its real motive is to compensate for this sense of weakness and lack. As a result, any "success" it wins will paradoxically reinforce the fact that it is weak and lacking: otherwise, why would it need to seek external goals? Only by going outside of itself can the ego appropriate those qualities it deems necessary to be seen as strong and whole.

This kicks off an endless cycle of searching as each "achievement" ultimately falls short of expectations. Worse yet, it exposes a deeper layer of need and launches the next round in the perpetual search. How could it be otherwise? How can what is inherently weak become strong? How can lack become fulfillment? How does nothing become something? A mirage will never harden into reality, no matter how doggedly you pursue it.

You already have a Self that was created by God. Nothing can replace this—especially not the nothingness that is the ego. There is no possible substitute or alternative for what is everything and always. Nor is there anything that can sully the purity or divide the wholeness of this Self that

---

* The ego's core sense of shame was a topic of the second book in this series, *From Loving One to One Love*.

God created. The ego's quest to improve its meager image of self is doomed from the start. That is also why it is never-ending.

Searches undertaken by the ego give rise to more searches, because its goals are unreal. The range of their results is bounded by the ego's inability to comprehend anything beyond its own nature. In the first book of this series, *From Never-Mind to Ever-Mind: Transforming the Self to Embrace Miracles*, I likened it to marooned sailors trying to quench their thirst with seawater. The more they drink, the more in need of water they become. Thirst leads to greater thirst. Lack leads to further lack.

No matter what the journey looks like or where it seems to be going, in truth there is only one destination that will satisfy—only one that delivers the pure water of spirit to our thirsting minds and brings our seeking to an end. This is the awakening to our true Self. Because this Self is never absent, never lost or separate from us, we realize at the journey's end that in fact there was no journey. As Dorothy discovered, it was all a bad dream.

The Journey through Space and Time

The ego's journey is an attempt to control uncertainty. The uncertainty is central to the ego's nature. The ego projects its frailty outside of itself in a futile attempt to free itself. This gives rise to the world in which we live. Because that frailty cannot be escaped through projection, it remains inherent in this world of the ego's making. It is a world populated by separate, individual bodies; a world defined by limitation and differences. The body itself is a limit on the expansive reality of spirit. It can exist only in one specific place at one particular time.

Our experience of space is limited to what our five senses bring to us. They perceive only a small fraction of the world. We can only mentally process a far smaller slice of whatever our senses focus on in a given moment. Watch TV, and you miss the sound of birds outside your window. Stare at your phone, and you miss pretty much everything. The five senses slice and dice the world into discrete objects and events. That which we see, hear, touch, taste, and smell becomes our world. There is no room for what lies beyond, and there is certainly no place for the vastness of spirit. What is limited cannot contain what has no limits.

Like space, time is also a limit: a limit on eternity. Time divides experience into past, present, and future (giving short shrift to the present). It further divides these into minutes, hours, days, and years.

Yet God is eternal and without limits of any kind. That is how he created us as well, as an extension of His Being. Time is therefore an attempt by the ego to limit God. This insane attempt gives rise to a world of insanity in which God and spirit are squeezed out. As long as we process experience in terms of time, they can play no role.

Because the ego's world is governed by the laws of space and time, so too are the journeys it undertakes. They may require it to travel someplace else—a journey through space. Alternately, they may require years of struggle and frustration while waiting for circumstances to change—a journey through time. Either way, the ego's journey plays out within its dream of separation. There is no visa, no green card, that can grant it admission to Heaven, where love is the only law, eternity the only "time," and God the only reality. The ego is condemned to walk the world it made and, within its limited confines, seek for what it regards as "salvation."

The problems with the ego's approach are many. But the most significant is this: Wherever we go and whoever we're with—however remarkable and amazing they may seem—we bring our old self along. We change the stage props, but not the play or the player. The body-based self is all we know (or so we believe). No matter how far we journey or whom we encounter, no matter how much riches or fame we accumulate, we do so as an ego-self. We remain enslaved to a false identity. And that's where the journey stalls. As I wrote in my book *From Plagues to Miracles: The Transformational Journey of Exodus, From the Slavery of Ego to the Promised Land of Spirit*:

> *The ego is crafty. It will gladly embrace a new set of roles and beliefs . . . to convince us we've changed, when all we've really done is rearrange the pieces of our self-concept. The slave exchanges one set of dirty clothing for another—and remains a slave. The truth is, we cannot use the ego-mind to free ourselves from ego. . . . A slave cannot escape using the tools of slavery.*[7]

After you've lived enough years, you begin to take notice of this pattern by which one ego goal falters and, before you have time to reconsider, another steps in to replace it.

It matters not how many times you end up hurt or disappointed; the ego always has another enticing bauble to dangle before your eyes and keep you seeking. Eventually you grow dispirited. Maybe you give up altogether. Maybe you resolve never to give up, determined to make good on the ego's promises no matter how long it takes. Or maybe you decide "there must be a better way," as Course coscribe Bill Thetford did. You abandon your prior efforts, along with the worldview on which they were based, and begin to look elsewhere for the answer to your discontent. You "*seek not outside yourself*,"[8] but instead look *inward*.

Who Are You?

Who are you? More to the point, *what* are you? How has your self-concept contributed to your problems? In what ways has it fueled your search and blocked you from finding real solutions? Only your true Self will satisfy. It lies within, waiting for you. But to find it, you must be willing to shed the false self you thought was you and all that goes with it.

As we've just seen, to the extent that you identify with the ego, your lot has been to seek outside yourself for what can only be found within. Even so, you cannot help but glean distant, fleeting glimpses of something greater that calls to you. This is because you *are* that something greater, and the resplendent truth of what you are cannot be entirely suppressed, however much the ego tries to do so. "*Truth is not absent here, but it is obscure.*"[9] For this reason, the journey of *A Course in Miracles* is not one of time or distance.

It can take a lifetime or transpire in a single instant. It is not a journey of discovery, because there is nothing outside you worth finding. It is a journey of recognition and self-knowledge. That is what you have lost. That is what you must reclaim.

> *There is no road that leads away from Him [God]. A journey from yourself does not exist. How foolish and insane it is to think that there could be a road with such an aim! Where could it go? And how could you be made to travel on it, walking there without your own reality at one with you?*[10]

The journey does not lead anywhere outside yourself, because nothing outside the Self exists. It is a journey through dreams to awakening, a journey of transformation. At the journey's end, you are no longer who or what you thought you were when you set out. You remember your identity as God's one creation, His Son. In that remembrance all else falls away and you return to the oneness of love and God, which in reality you never departed from.

> *You cannot lose your way because there is no way but His, and nowhere can you go except to Him.*[11]

> *When dreams are over, time has closed the door on all the things that pass and miracles are purposeless, the holy Son of God will make no journeys. There will be no wish to be illusion rather than the truth. And we step forth toward this, as we progress along the way that truth points out to us. This is our final journey, which we make for everyone.*[12]

2

Freedom

*You are not free to give up freedom, but only to deny it.
      You cannot do what God did not intend, because what
He did not intend does not happen.*[1]

Real freedom depends on welcoming reality.[2]

Freedom is a cherished ideal. Who among us doesn't want to be free? People have given up their lives in the struggle for freedom. The United States of America was founded on the principle of an individual's right to self-determination, that is, freedom from the tyranny of an oppressive monarch or government. The stereotype of the rugged, canny individual going it alone, cutting a path through all obstacles to achieve his desired goal, remains a staple of popular imagination. And yet those who founded the United States and blazed this trail of freedom were often slaveholders themselves.

This ugly paradox underscores just how relative freedom can be. If it is reserved for only a select few, then there is no freedom. In George Orwell's allegorical novel *Animal Farm*, the ruling pigs make it clear that, although in theory *all* animals are equal, *some* are more equal than others.

Given the opportunity, everyone would prefer to determine her own fate. Isn't this self-determination the essence of freedom? And yet how can we exercise such freedom if we don't know all the particulars of the situation we're involved in, down to its most subtle nuances? How can we make a rational judgment about what we want if we don't have the facts?

Take, for example, pharmaceutical products. There is a reason that most medications are available only with a doctor's prescription: the average person doesn't have the expertise to make an informed decision about what they may be putting into their bodies. They are susceptible to persuasion by hucksters. Doctors have the necessary knowledge but can be overruled by the government when a medication is determined to have unacceptable side effects. We accept this limit on our freedom, believing it is in our best interests. But to what extent does this hold true? What if a terminal patient is so desperate that she's willing to bear the risk of taking an unproven drug in hopes that it might prolong her life? Should she be denied? Who has the right to make that decision for her? Then again, what if her misinformed choice hastens her death? Who should be held responsible?

Along the same lines, should there be restrictions on recreational drugs like cannabis and alcohol—or even powerful intoxicants like cocaine, fentanyl, and heroin? How "free" should we be to indulge in whatever we choose, even if in the long term it will surely harm us?

The same question arises with greater urgency regarding firearms. Who should be free to own weapons that can potentially take the life of another? Where is the line between responsible sporting and hunting on the one hand and a credible risk of murder on the other? Are there limits to self-determination? If so, who gets to draw that line?

In each of these instances, one key question underlies the debate: does freedom serve the needs of the individual self or those of the collective society?

Most Americans would respond that freedom is about the individual self. However, this is hardly a universal belief. Most Chinese would echo Confucius and say that the good of society as a whole, and certainly of one's own extended family, takes precedence over the desires of any single individual within that family or society. But then we must ask, what leader has all the facts necessary to make sound policy for society as a whole? Who is so trustworthy and selfless that she can render perfect judgment over others' lives? Who has that right? After all, leaders themselves are individuals; the temptation to act in their own interests and those of their cronies forever pushes up against their desire to serve the public good.

As I noted in *From Never-Mind to Ever-Mind*, the key question is this: Which is the real "self"? Is it the individual who, along with other individuals, comprises the collective? Or is it the collective in which those individuals participate? Our answer will determine how we conceptualize freedom—whether it's for the individual or for society: for one or for all.

There is no right answer, of course. One man's freedom is another's bondage. If you are free to openly carry a handgun, then I am bound to feel afraid. Yet if I am to feel safe, then you are constrained from carrying a weapon in public, which in turn limits your freedom and leaves you feeling more afraid. Wars have been fought and lives taken in the name of different forms of "freedom."

In the ego's world, there is no way out of this dilemma, because each one believes that his or her own individual agenda is paramount. Freedom will always be relative—for one and not the other—as long as the perception of differences remains.

The Lessons of Exodus

In *From Plagues to Miracles*, I interpreted the biblical story of Moses, Pharaoh, and the Hebrews' escape from bondage in Egypt as a parable that charts the journey from slavery to freedom. Most understand this story purely in terms of release from physical bondage. If your body is imprisoned, if you are compelled to labor for another's benefit under fear of torture or death, you are a slave and have no freedom. The message of Exodus is that with God, freedom is not only possible, it is certain. Over the centuries, this message has inspired enslaved peoples everywhere to seek for their freedom.

At the start of Exodus, the Hebrews have been unfairly enslaved in Egypt under a new pharaoh. Moses is born to keep God's promise to His people and lead them to freedom. However, the journey is not a straightforward one. The Hebrew people cower at each obstacle in their path, repeatedly forgetting the promise made to them by God. They witness plagues that devastate the Egyptians, but leave them untouched. They experience the miraculous parting of the Red Sea (literally, the Sea of Reeds), which allows them to cross, but not the Egyptians, freeing them forever from Pharaoh and his armies. They are provided with sustenance in the form of manna, which reliably appears each morning for forty years while they wander the life-denying desert wilderness. Despite all of these miracles, they continue to grumble about how much better off they were in Egypt. Moses himself falters in his faith. Right from the outset, at the burning bush, he tries to squirm out of the mission God assigns to him. Later, when he leaves the Hebrews to ascend Mount Sinai and receive the Ten Commandments from God, they forge an idol, a golden calf. Moses grows so furious that he commands a purge that slaughters a quarter of his people. On the road to freedom, gratitude is scarce, fear, anger, recrimination, and second-guessing ever present.

The lessons of Exodus are many. God has promised to free us, His people (all of us, represented by the Hebrews). What must He free us from? What keeps us enslaved? The prison of the ego-mind and the world it weaves around us, the world of the five senses. God keeps His promises. But we cannot embrace freedom if we still cherish the ego, running to it for protection, obeying its commands, and trembling at the very thought of change. Our hands remain closed, unable to grasp what God so willingly offers. *"Freedom is offered them, but they have not accepted it, and what is offered must also be received, to be truly given."*[3]

Another lesson of Exodus is that the road to freedom is hard to follow, if not impossible, when you have no notion of what freedom looks like. How do you know you're free if you've never experienced anything of the kind? What's the endpoint? You may achieve freedom and, not realizing it, continue your search for something that will forever elude you. More likely, you will believe you've reached your Promised Land and stop searching when in fact you're nowhere near it. A prisoner who doesn't recognize the walls of her prison for what they are—who believes that she is already living a life of freedom within those walls—such a prisoner will make no effort to escape. Why would she? Escape from what? To what purpose?

Therefore, in order to achieve freedom, we first have to accept that *we don't know what it is.* We understand everything that happens to us in terms of our own limited experience—and that experience is defined by our imprisonment. We see all things "through a glass, darkly."[4] Therefore, any notion we cherish about what freedom should look like will be wrong. We don't know the way out. We're incapable of finding it on our own. We're too deep in dreaming.

I had a little dog, nineteen years old, deaf and blind and senile. He would wander around in circles trying to navigate his way through unexpected obstacles looking for his food dish or his bed. He'd bump into a chair or the wall, back up, start out again in a straight line . . . until he'd veer off course and smack into another obstacle. To him, the world was at best a maze, at worst a prison. I would help him out when I could. I'd use my feet to corral him, blocking his path when he began to drift off course, gradually channeling him toward his food. When I'd spy him desperately trying to reach the lawn to do his business, bumping into bushes and bouncing off the legs of lawn chairs, I would lift him up and carry him, gently depositing him on the grass.

To that little dog, I was a source of miracles. I helped him clear away the obstacles and get to where he wanted to go. But I didn't always know what he wanted. I was making assumptions based on limited information: what I could see and what I inferred based on past experience. There were many times I saw him wandering around the patio and lifted him to the grass, assuming he needed to pee, only to have him turn right around because he'd already peed and was actually trying to find his way back to the house. In those instances, I wasn't helping; I was setting him back.

Human beings are not so different from my dog. It's known that people lost in the woods inevitably wander in circles. They believe they're making progress—until they stumble upon the same clearing with the same fallen tree and realize they've spent hours going nowhere. We don't really know how to get where we want to go. We can't find our way out of the woods, either literally or metaphorically.

To escape the ego's prison, we need help, help that seems to come from outside ourselves. We need an airlift onto the soft grass or a gentle redirect away from false goals toward what we really want. We need a guide to keep us from deviating and meandering in useless circles—a Moses to deliver miracles that lead us to the Promised Land. *A Course in Miracles* calls this guide the *Holy Spirit*, and He is available to each of us in every moment because He lives within us, in our minds. If he appears to be an outside force, it is only because we've lost our way so badly.

Therefore, to find freedom we don't need to *do* anything specific. Actions we undertake on our own are misguided. Instead, we need to train our minds to ask for His help in every circumstance, listen to the answer we're given, and follow that guidance. It can come in many forms. It can be vague and general or highly detailed and specific. Either way, we learn that we do not have to go it alone—that in truth there is no such thing as *alone*. As God tells Moses at the burning bush (three times, no less!), "I will be with you." We are never absent from God and the Holy Spirit because They are our only reality. We can misplace things of value, we can lose our way and even our very identities here in the world, but we can never lose God. Little children take delight in playing peekaboo. They cover their eyes and—oh, no!—their beloved mother is gone! They open their eyes again and squeal in delight, "There she is!" Because in reality she never left.

The Holy Spirit's gentle guidance feels miraculous to us, but it's the most natural thing in the world—perhaps the *only* natural thing in this world. It undercuts our existential fear and greatly shortens the time we waste in wandering. It may seem ironic that the most direct path to what we want requires us to follow guidance. To the ego, this is sacrilege. What goal could be worth surrendering our precious autonomy? Better to strive and fight on, even if it gets us nowhere. And so we do. That is the problem with the ego's vision of freedom: it gets us nowhere.

The Myth of Choice

We tend to imagine freedom as unlimited, unconstrained choice. We get to do whatever we want. The world opens before us—a menu of infinite variety—inviting us to explore all the wonderful dishes it has to offer. No one tells us what to order: what we should do or how to go about it. We are free to choose.

Where do you want to live? With whom? What kind of car do you prefer? What will you eat for dinner? Watch on Netflix? This field of unlimited choice seems very appealing. Psychology has demonstrated, however, that an abundance of choice is not necessarily a good thing. It becomes overwhelming, even paralyzing. When confronted with a decision that involves more than three or four options, we begin to question our choices. We flit from one to the next, weighing the pros and cons, never certain which is right for us, which will truly satisfy. When we do arrive at a decision, it is too often subject to buyer's remorse. In retrospect, we should have made a different choice. We should have known better. Yet that choice too would have fallen prey to second-guessing.

In order to make a good choice, we think that what we need is information: the more, the better. Without information there is no basis for decision. This seems self-evident, but the need for information turns out to be more problematic than it first appears. What information is relevant? From what source? Who's trustworthy? Think about the last time you shopped Amazon's website for a particular item, trying to ascertain which brand was best by reading all the reviews for each one. How long did it take you? How confident were you in your final choice? Did you wonder whether perhaps, with more time, you might have made a better choice? A more "informed" choice? Or did you just give up and go with your gut?

A Course in Miracles tells us that no matter the circumstances, there is only one choice confronting us—ever. It is the choice between the ego and the Holy Spirit. Whose voice do we listen to? Which we choose will determine whether we seek reality or dreams, peace or strife, love or fear. Remember, the journey's one and only goal is to awaken to our true nature: the Self that God created. This Self needs nothing and has everything because, as spirit, it was created to *be* everything. Only this Self leads to happiness.

Choice among illusions is not freedom, nor is it really choice. It is deception: a three-card monte scam that's rigged against you. You pick a card; you're wrong. You pick another. Wrong again! You repeatedly swap one false choice for another. Your choices may appear to be different, with a far wider range than three playing cards. But they all exist within the same framework of illusion. Therefore, they are equally unreal.

The problem is that we have been taught to regard freedom as something that the ego is capable of delivering to us. It is freedom understood in terms of the body: go anywhere, do anything, get the things you want for yourself. But the body is a limit on freedom. Its needs and desires are designed to keep us imprisoned. You cannot free yourself by piling on more chains.

> *Do you want freedom of the body or of the mind? For both you cannot have. Which do you value? Which is your goal? . . . No one but yearns for freedom and tries to find it. Yet he will seek for it where he believes it is and can be found. He will believe it possible of mind or body, and he will make the other serve his choice as means to find it.*
>
> *Where freedom of the body has been chosen, the mind is used as means whose value lies in its ability to contrive ways to achieve the body's freedom. Yet freedom of the body has no meaning, and so the mind is dedicated to serve illusions.*[5]

Each choice we make with the ego represents a decision to value something more than truth, more than God. We pursue that goal as if it were the only true god, but we are really worshiping idols. It's no wonder we're left dissatisfied! To choose idols is to choose *not* to awaken: to keep dreaming. It's like an alcoholic who can't decide whether to switch from vodka to beer or hang out at a different bar in order to quit drinking.

Of course, life confronts us with a seemingly endless number of decisions to be made. Every day and every hour we are choosing between different options: which clothes to wear, what to eat, which bill to pay first, and so on. We can get very tied up in these choices, but most of them are trivial and not worth a great deal of thought. Whether you start your day with coffee, tea, or orange juice is probably of little consequence to your spiritual growth. When faced with the bigger, more difficult choices, however—like how to respond to someone who's hurt you, someone you love and care about—we must learn *not* to rely on our own judgment.

Our decisions are invariably based on the results of past choices. If whatever we did seemed to work out, we're likely to do it again. If it did not, we'll try something else. Maybe we'll seek more information. But as the Course points out, we never see the entire picture. We're incapable of that, because the ego-mind is limited. It was made by separation, and it is defined by separation. The ego weighs one select piece of data against another without regard for unseen connections, hidden qualifiers, subtle nuances, and the greater whole within which everything plays out. The ego cannot be aware of any of these. As a result, no matter how much data we gather, our choices must remain biased and blind. Understanding this, we can make only one decision that is guaranteed to lead us in the right direction: we can *decide against deciding* on our own and choose instead to listen to the Holy Spirit.

Before you make any decisions for yourself, remember that you have decided against your function in Heaven, and then consider carefully whether you want to make decisions here. Your function here is only to decide against deciding what you want, in recognition that you do not know. How, then, can you decide what you should do? Leave all decisions to the One Who speaks for God [the Holy Spirit]. . . .

> *When you have learned how to decide with God, all decisions become as easy and as right as breathing. There is no effort, and you will be led as gently as if you were being carried down a quiet path in summer.*[6]

Stop and consider this image of being carried down a quiet path in summer. Can you feel the peace it brings? You exert no effort, because you made the one right choice: the choice to be led by guidance. Like my dog, you allow yourself to be carried along by a gentle, caring being far wiser than yourself. Remember if you can what it felt like to be carried in the arms of someone loving. Most of us lose this experience of safety past the age of five, when we grow too big to be carried. But isn't this a feeling you would want? Isn't this a better alternative than collecting as much information as possible in hopes of making the "right" choice?

What we thought we desired and called by the name of freedom—the ability to decide for ourselves from amongst limitless choices—turns out to be just the opposite. When we try to make decisions on our own, using our own "best judgment," we set ourselves an impossible task. But when we turn instead to the One Who *does* see the whole picture, the Holy Spirit, and ask Him to guide us, we are freed from this burden. The Holy Spirit knows only truth, only light, only love. That's all He sees in you or me or anyone. Therefore, the path He chooses for us must inevitably lead to those outcomes. To find happiness, love, truth, and peace, make the only choice that really means anything. Make the choice for truth, not another form of illusion. Choose to follow Him.

The Comforts of Prison Life

We noted earlier that in order to escape from prison, you must first understand that you are in fact a prisoner. If your prison is beautifully adorned, if it comes with all the amenities, if it fans your desires with countless temptations, then you will not recognize it for what it is. It will never occur to you to escape.

This situation is depicted metaphorically in the 1999 film *The Matrix*, which portrays the world we inhabit as a virtual reality computer simulation designed to harness our energy while keeping us comatose.

The same idea was explored decades earlier in what was intended to be the pilot episode for the original Star Trek series.* A race of aliens is able to telepathically manipulate human perception in order to hold a woman and a starship captain in captivity. They fall in love, of course, and survive many challenges together. Eventually, the captain figures out the aliens' ruse and forces them to reveal reality as it is. The truth turns out to be ugly and unsettling. But the story is told in flashback from a point where the captain has become totally paralyzed. In a brilliant stroke of irony, he begs to be returned to the alien planet, where in his mind he can roam free, unfettered by his damaged physical body and joined by the woman he loves. They can live out their lives together, happily immersed in illusion.

---

* This pilot episode of *Star Trek* was originally titled "The Cage." Renamed "The Menagerie," it aired as the eleventh and twelfth episodes in the show's first season in 1966.

We are a lot like that starship captain. We too relish living in illusion—except that unlike him, we have forgotten that this was a choice we made. To regain freedom, it is essential to see our prison for what it is and what it is not.

There are many ways in which we allow ourselves to become enslaved to illusion. We can become captive to possessions. Misplace your mobile phone, and you'll see just how much you've bartered your freedom for its conveniences. We can be captive to the acquisition of riches, believing that our salvation lies in the size of our bank account. We are certainly captive to the physical body: maintaining its health, treating its infirmities, chasing after its pleasures, and minimizing its suffering. Our long-held beliefs and even our cherished values can become heavy chains that we refuse to cast off. The same is true for the many different roles we play throughout life: child, parent, lover, friend, student, professional. We embrace these as if they were part of us. When we are forced to shed them, it is usually with a sense of loss and much suffering. Taken together, they forge what we think of as our *self*. But it is a false self, and a highly unstable one. It is always changing, adjusting to what it regards as forces external to itself, like going to a new school, being dumped by a boyfriend, being laid off, divorcing, retiring, and the most difficult of all: dealing with the death of someone you love, and ultimately, your own death. As long as we buy into this self-concept, believing that it is us, change and suffering will be our fate.

A Prisoner of Expectations

From a very early age, we are taught that one of the most important things in life—perhaps the thing that will most determine whether we are happy or miserable—is our choice of a romantic partner. We craft an ideal image of this person based on what we see in others and, increasingly, what we take in from media and social media. That rap star seems to have a great life with a hot relationship; that's what I want. The happy ending of the romcom is too tempting to refuse. As a result, we are constantly scanning those around us for partner material and auditioning anyone we're attracted to for the role. But our expectations are high. Reality almost never lives up them. Yet each break up opens the door to new possibilities. As we saw in chapter 1, the ego will keep us searching. Like the prince and Cinderella, one day we will find the right one, and the shoe will fit.

For some, the idea of such a partner is terrifying, something to be avoided at all costs—whether through isolation, pursuing goals like work or sports, or, paradoxically, by having as many relationships as possible. They follow the trail of attraction, flitting from one person to the next, never settling, because to settle is to forgo all the other opportunities you would have. If the grass is always greener in someone else's pasture, you never have to settle. You never risk real hurt or rejection. You move on before anyone has a chance to see deeply into who you are. You may tell everyone, including yourself, that you're just looking for the right person, but in fact that's the last thing you want. The search becomes more compelling than what it pretends to find.

The quest for the ideal partner is another of the ego's mirages. There is no such thing. There is nobody out there sunning themselves on some tropical beach, biding their time, just waiting for you to stroll into their life and make it all worthwhile. Good relationships are not like precious gems lying in the dirt, waiting to be discovered. They are forged in the fires of daily life, hardened by the pressures of conflict and resolution, until they emerge diamondlike, shimmering. It takes time to understand that the crucible of a relationship makes us better. That's why we commit; that's why the work is so essential and ultimately so rewarding.

When you first meet someone, you build a mental picture that's very sketchy. It's part fantasy, part inference, spiced with maybe a dash of honest observation. From this heavily Photoshopped image, you develop expectations. These are based on your ideal image of what a partner should be. They are also reflections of past relationships you've known, both the good and the bad, including your parents. Did your dad always kiss your mom in the morning? Then so should your partner. But if your dad never kissed anyone under any circumstances, then why would your partner expect that from you? Did your ex control the remote? Your next will never set fingers on that device.

Each expectation becomes a chain that binds both you and your partner. If the expectation is met, that's terrific. But you'll expect them to be met again in the future. Your partner will inevitably fail to live up to some expectation of yours, however, and then you will feel disappointed or angry. You're far more likely to blame them than question the basis for your own expectation. Your ideal image of them begins to erode, shifting from "good" to "bad," providing you with further justification for your resentment. You feel increasingly like a prisoner in the relationship until finally there seems to be no other choice except to leave. But you were never held prisoner by them, only by your own mental expectations.

Relationships can serve as vehicles for freedom or oppression. How we see them is what they will become.

The Past as Prison

We go through life spinning an endless web of expectations about what should happen, a web that entraps us. Some expectations are perfectly reasonable. The sun will rise in the morning and set at night. If you drive someplace like work or the grocery store, you expect to arrive and return safely. You anticipate birthdays and holidays arriving according to the calendar. Accidents can happen, but unless you're suffering from an anxiety disorder, these are not part of your expectations. By contrast, if you expect your children to behave a certain way, to share your goals and values, then your expectations will most likely be challenged.

Expectations rely on judgments. We prefer one outcome over another. We judge them in terms of which is best, which will lead to the greatest happiness. We are often wrong, because judgment is a function of the past.

We compare current circumstances with what happened before. How else would we know what to seek and what to avoid? Did you have a good meal at that restaurant? Then you'll go there again and recommend it to your friends. Did you get violently ill afterwards? You'll never go near the place, even though medically the odds are that you contracted a stomach virus, not food poisoning. In making judgments then, we establish the past as the arbiter of what's happening now. It's the metric against which we measure all experience. The result is that we become its willing prisoners.

We take the past (however we remember it) and overlay it on the current situation in order to make sense of it. What worked before should work again, we reason, while what did not work isn't worth repeating. We reached out to pet the growling dog; it bit us; we will not pet growling dogs again. As a result, we never see dogs in the same way. Our perception of dogs is colored by our past experience.

We didn't really understand the past even when it occurred. There were too many variables, too many unseen forces that lay well beyond our capacity to comprehend. Who knows why that dog reacted as it did? Was it mistreated? Starving? Bred to be vicious? Or perhaps it was just startled when we tried to touch it.

Misunderstanding increases when it hardens into a memory. Recall is selective, focusing on certain aspects of what happened; some features grow more prominent, while others, which may have been more important, fade into the background. As a result, our expectations for what could happen in the future are skewed.

The future is simultaneously dangerous and alluring. It's that field of wide-open potential where the good things we desire may finally come true, but also where misfortune lies in wait in the form of illness, accidents, failure, losses of all kinds, and death. We try to anticipate the future on the basis of the past, but fear it because we know it is unknown. Nonetheless, we do our best to control the future. We make plans to tame its wild uncertainties. We save up funds for a rainy day. We take vitamins and herbal supplements. We buy insurance.

In this way, past and future become the concrete walls of the ego's prison. As long as we give credence to their reality and rely on the one to protect us from the other, we leave no opening for real change.

The past is over. It is fixed and inflexible. It cannot change. The only thing it offers is a false sense of predictability. The future is yet to be. It is uncertain, imaginary. It cannot be pinned down, however much we try. Every time we turn our thoughts to it, it shifts again. In this sense, it is always changing. But change that does not last—change that gives way to another and yet another change—is not *real* change. You remain the same self. You may think you're wiser as a result of experience, but you're kidding yourself. Your past binds you to it and guarantees that your future will hold no release.

Between past and future lies eternity. That's right: eternity. We call it the present, but we seldom consider what that means. The present is always exactly as it is. It cannot be altered or held hostage by the past or the future. Past and future are determined by their content. What happened in the past? What will happen in the future? They are like cluttered rooms, storage lockers tightly packed with all the things we think about: fears, dreams, preoccupations.

Not so the present. It is independent of content. Each time we experience it, it is the same: unchanged and unchangeable. It is not possible to experience the pure present while retaining any thought of the past or future. Focus on either and the present vanishes from sight. It is still there, still *present*, but you will no longer know it.

The present is the doorway that leads out of the ego's prison. It opens wide onto the fresh air of truth and happiness. It has no content: no constraints or limits. And the peculiar thing—the obvious thing that we somehow overlook day in and day out—is that it is with us all the time. It is always there, always *present*. We live and move in it. There *is* nothing else. Every moment is now. All of time is now. We live in eternity, but act as if it weren't there.

Can you grasp the power of this idea? The ego's prison walls are not simply full of holes called "the present" through which you can dart at any moment. The truth reveals that *there are no walls*, except of our own making. They do not exist. The present is unbound. It is the gateway to freedom: "the gateless gate" (to borrow from the famous Zen koan). It is the escape route from our own entrapped mind. We cannot avoid it. This open invitation to freedom stands in wait for us in every moment, with every breath. We can't change it; we can only look away, groaning under the weight of the heavy chains of past and future in which we've bound ourselves. Eternity beckons. You *will* awaken to it. That's never in doubt. It is your birthright. It's only a matter of time.

The Prisoners of Perception

Like *The Matrix* and the *Star Trek* pilot, *A Course in Miracles* teaches that the world we perceive through our five senses—the ego's world—is nothing but illusion. It is the miscreation of our own mind. It is a world defined by separation. We see separate objects; we encounter separate bodies with their distinct personalities; and we experience discreet events that seem to happen to us, as if inflicted from outside, beyond our power to control. It is a world of limits. We experience this as a limitation on our physical and cognitive abilities. We are not infinitely strong or infinitely intelligent. What we accomplish is constricted, not only by our own shortcomings, but ultimately by aging and death. All that lives must die.

These are limits we recognize, even if we prefer not to think of them. However, we seldom question the limited nature of perception itself. We are capable of viewing galaxies hundreds of millions of light-years distant, but we cannot peer into infinity. In the world of the senses, infinity is an abstraction that does not exist. There is always a limit to what can be perceived. In fact, the moment we perceive *anything*, we make it finite.

That which limits also imprisons. If you are bound by limits of any kind, you cannot claim perfect freedom. In a very real sense, then, the world we inhabit is a prison, and perception is the guardian that keeps its walls seemingly solid and unbreachable. Perception keeps our focus fixed upon what is *not* there. As a result, we do not see what *is* present and real. We do not see anyone as they truly are.

If you wanted to enter a virtual reality simulation, you would need some kind of image of self—an *avatar*—in order to interact and move about within its world. It could be the image of you as you now see yourself, only improved: prettier, stronger, taller. Or you might choose to be represented by someone or something else. You could be Joan of Arc, Superman, Cleopatra, a Siamese cat, or a scaly dragon. If you remain in the VR world long enough, you risk forgetting your "real" self. You begin to identify with your avatar in the simulation as if *it* were the real you. You become captive to this image of self *that you chose*, and this in turn makes your experience of the simulated reality all the more immediate and compelling. But the image, the avatar, is not *you*, nor will it ever be. It's a convenient placeholder within the VR world: the point from which your virtual perception extends outward. It is no more real than any other aspect of that world. But as long as you can see it and feel it, as long as you invest belief in what you see and feel, it will define you. It becomes a self-willed, self-contained prison.

The Course tells us that the ego's world is nothing more than a very vivid VR-like illusion. Therefore, the self that lives within that world, the self that identifies with a physical body, the self we all have and know, is also an illusion. To awaken, it is necessary to expose both the world of perception and the self that perceives it as illusions, then to pierce them and ultimately to break free of them.

People have attempted to escape from the world of perception since time began. The senses begin to break down when focused on one fixed percept: a candle flame, a bonfire, the vastness of the ocean or a field of stars, the rhythm of the breath moving in and out of the body. Drumming, dancing, and whirling likewise destabilize the senses. Certain drugs like mescaline (found in the peyote cactus), psilocybin (from certain species of mushrooms), cannabis, and LSD distort the senses or blow them out entirely. They open the mind to a realization of the frailty of the world of the senses, as if it were the thinnest skin stretched across the face of truth and blocking it from our sight.

Yet drugs wear off, meditation comes to an end, and we return to the world of perception. It enfolds us within its compelling contours. Our body-based avatar self takes charge once again. The experience of beingness that we had when we shed the chains of perception hardens into a memory and loses its power to transform.

A Course in Miracles has a great deal to say about the nature of perception and its origins (see also chapter 2 of my book *From Never-Mind to Ever-Mind*):

> *Perception seems to teach you what you see. Yet it but witnesses to what you taught. It is the outward picture of a wish: an image that you wanted to be true.*[7]

> *Perception is a choice of what you want yourself to be; the world you want to live in, and the state in which you think your mind will be content and satisfied. It chooses where you*

*think your safety lies, at your decision. It reveals yourself to
you as you would have you be.*[8]

*Perception is a mirror, not a fact. And what I look on is my
state of mind, reflected outward.*[9]

The point is not subtle. We are prisoners of perception only
because we choose to be. And yet here we find ourselves.
We built the prison, locked ourselves within its illusory
walls, did our best to forget where we hid the key, and went
deeper into illusion, forgetting that such imprisonment was
even possible. As a result, escape seems impossible, even if
we wanted it—which most do not. As we've said before,
there is no longer anything to escape from. We are locked
in the Matrix, ignorant of our true state and with little
desire to take even the smallest step toward freedom, much
less escape fully.

If we were somehow to escape from this prison of perception, what would we see instead? What is the opposite
of perception? It's difficult to conceptualize, because pretty
much everything we know comes from what we've learned
through the five senses.

The Course says that perception's opposite is "knowledge" (as long as we understand that what is nonexistent
can have no real opposite). It gives this word a very specific
meaning. Knowledge applies only to the realm of God and
His creation, because that is the only reality. Knowledge
is equivalent to being. It is an aspect of being. You *know*
because you *are*. The two are inseparable, indistinguishable.
There is no intermediary between being and knowing as

there is with perception, because how can anything mediate between oneness and what is still oneness? What can come between oneness and itself? Perception requires separation. There must be distance between subject and object. This provides a perspective that's unique to you, the observer, and not shared with the observed. By contrast, knowledge is unitary. It cannot be separated, subdivided, or viewed from outside itself. Nothing exists outside this Self.

How do we begin to undo perception and free ourselves from its limits in order to welcome back the realm of knowledge? It's not easy. Our infancy and childhood were devoted to mastering perception. We had to learn how to see, hear, and speak clearly; to identify objects and manipulate them; to make inferences about how people and things behave based on how they behaved in the past. How do we begin now to unwind all of this?

We cannot manage it on our own because we remain prisoners of the dream we made. "*The dreamer of a dream is not awake, but does not know he sleeps.*"[10] More problematic still, our dream identity—our virtual reality avatar—is itself part of the dream. "*Identity in dreams is meaningless because the dreamer and the dream are one.*"[11] To awaken from the dream is to lose your identity, which is the only one you know anymore. Therefore the idea of awakening is terrifying. To the ego, awakening is the equivalent of death: the loss of its identity as a body. If awakening means dying, who would want it?

We've also gotten used to living in prison. We've accepted it and adapted. We have become "institutionalized," and prefer the predictable routine of prison life to whatever the alternative might be. Better the devil you know . . .

Therefore we cannot awaken on our own. We cannot free ourselves from the prison of perception, because we made it, we still believe in it, and that belief actively maintains it. Nor can we use our false self to reclaim our true one. As long as the false ego-self dominates, our true Self must remain out of reach.

To awaken, we need help: a boost, a rescue line, a loving guide who can take us by the hand and lead us safely to where we would otherwise dare not go. As the Course says many times, this help is waiting and it is ever present. It is the Holy Spirit. He is the mediator between the false and the true, the bridge between illusion and reality. His function is to filter perception in such a way that only what is aligned with God and truth is seen. Only your loving thoughts are real. All else is worthless illusion.

The Holy Spirit doesn't have to vanquish or destroy what is unreal. That would paradoxically make it seem more real. He only has to look past it to the truth, and it is no more. The Course calls this process "forgiveness." It is our only purpose here in the ego's prison of perception. It is our way out.

You are not in charge of this process. You place yourself in the Holy Spirit's hands. Ideally, you become as a little child, trusting in Him and certain that His direction is what you would choose for yourself. But you do have a role to play, and it is essential. You must bring to Him all of your thoughts and perceptions, the entire past as you know it, for Him to sort out. You remove the blocks to the awareness of love's presence by first becoming aware of them and then, when ready, gently releasing them.

> *To forgive is merely to remember only the loving thoughts you gave in the past, and those that were given you. All the rest must be forgotten. Forgiveness is a selective remembering, based not on your selection.*[12]

> *Your part is very simple. You need only recognize that everything you learned you do not want. Ask to be taught, and do not use your experience to confirm what you have learned. When your peace is threatened or disturbed in any way, say to yourself:*
>   *I do not know what anything, including this, means. And so I do not know how to respond to it. And I will not use my own past learning as the light to guide me now.*[13]

Forgiveness is not so much a process of learning as unlearning. We demote the value of our own judgments in favor of the Holy Spirit's. We understand that if we judge, we reinforce the value of the past in our minds. This keeps us dreaming. Instead, we develop the habit of relinquishing what we think about a given situation to the Holy Spirit and His judgment. As Workbook lessons 20–21 and 27–28 affirm, we want to see differently. We want to shift our perception such that it no longer reinforces separation, but frees us from it.

This process almost always takes time. If release is too abrupt, it provokes fear, which is antithetical to the Holy Spirit's mission. He cannot lead you if you are afraid, because fear does not exist in His reality. Fear reinforces separation and strengthens our ties to illusion. It's what He is here to release you from. By definition, then, the Holy Spirit is incapable of bringing to you anything you would find fearful. He knows your readiness and brings you only what you can willingly look at and release without fear. This is a progressively evolving curriculum. It is tailored to your needs and proceeds at a pace that's most effective for you. Your role is to comply—to take the next step, and then the next—without concern for where you're headed or demanding to go faster.

Here's the key to allowing this: *the Holy Spirit is you.* He is the reflection of your true Self, the Christ, within the dream. He is the memory, so to speak, or the imprint, of your reality, which can never be lost. You're having a bad nightmare; within the nightmare you feel a gentle tug that lets you know you are dreaming and calls you to awaken. When you open your eyes, you see the smiling face of someone who loves you. She recognized that you were trapped in a bad dream and helped you to escape from it. Think of the Holy Spirit as that someone, only much more. He is the pure love of God shining through the prison walls of perception. He can pass right through what you thought was solid and impenetrable, thereby demonstrating to you that it is not. It's no more than a dream, and you are now free to awaken.

Awakening to the Real World

I said earlier that the opposite of perception is knowledge. However, as long as we believe we're here, inside a body, we cannot attain the state of knowledge. The body is a limit. It is finite. Knowledge is infinite, limitless. They cannot coexist.

Recall that we are like institutionalized prisoners, no longer capable of attaining freedom, or even of understanding it. We need to undergo a rehabilitation program, an interval in which we continue to use perception in a different way—not to bind, but to release. We trust that knowledge will be ours when we are fully ready to embrace it, but in the meantime, it would be good to acclimate.

> *Prisoners bound with heavy chains for years, starved and emaciated, weak and exhausted, and with eyes so long cast down in darkness they remember not the light, do not leap up in joy the instant they are made free. It takes a while for them to understand what freedom is.*[14]

Because you have lived in the ego's prison your entire life, it is almost impossible to return directly to knowledge. The fear of death is too strong. Even the tiniest investment in separation will hold you back. *"One illusion cherished and defended against the truth makes all truth meaningless, and all illusions real."*[15] We need to experience the world of perception purified of the ego's judgments and the past. We must see it in a whole new light, one in which our holiness shines forth and separation has no more meaning. As Workbook lesson 313 affirms, *"Now let a new perception come to me"*:

> *Father, there is a vision which beholds all things as sinless, so that fear has gone, and where it was is love invited in. And love will come wherever it is asked. . . .*

Let us today behold each other in the sight of Christ.
How beautiful we are! How holy and how loving![16]

This is Christ's vision, which reveals what the Course calls "the real world." It is a beautiful concept, but unfortunately, one that students find among the most confusing. Why? Because the real world is not real in the sense that God, Christ and the Holy Spirit are real. It was not created by God. It is the world of perception cleansed of all perception's judgments and offered to the Holy Spirit. It is not Heaven, but it is so close to Heaven that God can easily cross and meet us there, where He will take "the final step" and return us to our true Identity as Christ. We have removed all of the obstacles that stood in the way of this and so it becomes the most natural thing in the world. Maybe the *only* truly natural thing.

We receive glimpses of the real world long before we make it our permanent vision. These are the mystical moments I described in chapter 3 of *From Never-Mind to Ever-Mind*, along with the conditions that give rise to them. Picture if you can a world without fear, or even the possibility of fear. Picture a world suffused with soft, gentle light. You move through this world with an enduring sense of peacefulness. Nothing can disturb it, nor is it related in any way to the circumstances of your life, by which you once felt victimized and which you once strived mightily to control.

It is the Bible's "peace of God, which passeth all understanding."[17] It is the Promised Land, understood not as an actual geographic location, but as a metaphor for a state of mind in which peace and love are paramount. There is no more struggle, no need to strategize or plan. Your needs—such as they are—are met completely, often in unexpected ways that you never could have brought about on your own. You no longer judge; you have no need to. You follow the guidance and you receive its gifts. You share those gifts with whomever the Holy Spirit brings your way. You understand that your interests and theirs are the same because there is no separation between you. What you give you receive back tenfold, and what you receive extends out to all those who hunger for peace, joy, love, a sense of real purpose, and the dawning memory of God.

The Course tells us that before we return to the Self that God created one with Him—the Christ—we will experience the real world. It is not real in the ultimate sense. It is still anchored to perception, but that perception is no longer being employed in the service of judgment and separation. It is the world of perception cleansed of our judgments. We may still be in prison, but its bars and locks are gone, dissolved through our forgiveness. The doors and windows are gaping open, allowing the fresh breezes of freedom to blow through. We can stroll out at any time.

You will first dream of peace, and then awaken to it. Your first exchange of what you made for what you want is the exchange of nightmares for the happy dreams of love. In these lie your true perceptions, for the Holy Spirit corrects the world of dreams, where all perception is. Knowledge needs no correction. Yet the dreams of love lead unto knowledge. In them you see nothing fearful, and because of this they are

*the welcome that you offer knowledge. Love waits on wel-
come, not on time, and the real world is but your welcome of
what always was. Therefore the call of joy is in it, and your
glad response is your awakening to what you have not lost.*[18]

*Can you imagine how beautiful those you forgive will look
to you? In no fantasy have you ever seen anything so lovely.
Nothing you see here, sleeping or waking, comes near to such
loveliness. And nothing will you value like unto this, nor
hold so dear. Nothing that you remember that made your
heart sing with joy has ever brought you even a little part of
the happiness this sight will bring you. . . .*

*This loveliness is not a fantasy. It is the real world, bright
and clean and new, with everything sparkling under the
open sun. Nothing is hidden here, for everything has been
forgiven and there are no fantasies to hide the truth. . . .*

*The real world is attained simply by the complete for-
giveness of the old, the world you see without forgiveness.*[19]

As appealing as it is, the real world is only a way station on
the journey back to God. You are not yet free of your body,
although your identification with it is very loose. You could
shed it in an instant with no hesitancy or regret, because you
know it is not *you*. As we noted, the real world still relies on
perception, and perception is unreal. This is the paradox of
the so-called "real world," which makes it such a confusing
concept. It is as real as the world can get, but still it is not
real in any ultimate sense. It is not the oneness of God.

You are not a body, and you do not live within a world
of bodies and things. You are spirit. As long as you iden-

tify with the body, its loss will feel like a sacrifice. This is the misinterpretation that was applied to the crucifixion of Jesus of Nazareth. He had to sacrifice his body to free us of sin. But if the body is unreal, then where is the sacrifice? The loss of nothing cannot be sacrifice. To experience this, however, you must already know that your true Self has nothing to do with a body. It is spirit. "*Spirit am I, a holy Son of God, free of all limits, safe and healed and whole, free to forgive and free to save the world.*"[20]

Spirit is eternal. Spirit cannot die, because it was not born. It exists within the Being of its Creator, within which is all reality. The understanding of this sets us on the road to freedom, but the to experience it *is* freedom. When we remember that we are spirit, no different from any of our brothers or sisters and no different from God, we are free. In that instant we also know that we have always been free. There are no chains, no dreams, no illusions, that can imprison God's Son, because He is spirit.

To find freedom, there is only one choice we must make, one decision to work towards with the help of the Holy Spirit. Are you the limited being that you believe yourself to be? Are you an ego mind with private thoughts? Do you navigate your physical body through a forbidding external world over which you have little control, seeking rare moments of satisfaction and pleasure? Are you a prisoner of time in which your future is modeled on what you learned in the past? If any of these are true, then freedom cannot come. You have not allowed it. The door to freedom stands open, but you refuse to see it.

Or are you spirit, created by God as an extension of His Being: an infinite, eternal presence that is free to dream it is imprisoned, but cannot change the fundamental nature of its reality?

Which are you? Which do you *want* to be your real self? This is the only decision that faces you, and the only one that brings about real freedom.

Salvation does not ask that you behold the spirit and perceive the body not. It merely asks that this should be your choice. For you can see the body without help, but do not understand how to behold a world apart from it. It is your world salvation will undo, and let you see another world your eyes could never find.[21]

The real world still is but a dream. Except the figures have been changed. They are not seen as idols which betray. It is a dream in which no one is used to substitute for something else, nor interposed between the thoughts the mind conceives and what it sees. No one is used for something he is not, for childish things have all been put away. And what was once a dream of judgment now has changed into a dream where all is joy, because that is the purpose that it has. Only forgiving dreams can enter here, for time is almost over. And the forms that enter in the dream are now perceived as brothers, not in judgment, but in love.[22]

There is no one who does not feel that he is imprisoned in some way. If this is the result of his own free will he must regard his will as not free, or the circular reasoning in this position would be quite apparent. Free will must lead to freedom. Judgment always imprisons because it separates segments of reality by the unstable scales of desire. Wishes are not facts.[23]

How wonderful it is to do your will! For that is freedom. There is nothing else that should ever be called by freedom's name. Unless you do your will you are not free.[24]

You do not really want the world you see, for it has disappointed you since time began. The homes you built have never sheltered you. The roads you made have led you nowhere, and no city that you built has withstood the crumbling assault of time. Nothing you made but has the mark of death upon it. Hold it not dear, for it is old and tired and ready to return to dust even as you made it. This aching world has not the power to touch the living world at all. You could not give it that, and so although you turn in sadness from it, you cannot find in it the road that leads away from it into another world.

Yet the real world has the power to touch you even here, because you love it. And what you call with love will come to you. Love always answers, being unable to deny a call for help, or not to hear the cries of pain that rise to it from every part of this strange world you made but do not want. All that you need to give this world away in glad exchange for what you did not make is willingness to learn the one you made is false.[25]

3

The Body

The body is the symbol of the ego, as the ego is the symbol of the separation.[1]

The Christ in you inhabits not a body. Yet He is in you. And thus it must be that you are not within a body.[2]

For just a moment, stop reading and take a good look at yourself. Do it now, then return to the book.

What did you see? If you're like most people, you looked at your physical body. Maybe at your hands or your torso. Or perhaps you put the book down and glanced at your face in a mirror. It would seem to be the most natural response in the world, and yet, according to *A Course in Miracles*, there's nothing natural about it whatsoever.

You identify with your physical body; that is a fact. You think it's *you*. But it's not that simple. I doubt that anyone looked down at their toes, for instance, and thought, "That's me!" You select certain features, certain aspects that you like or dislike, and appoint these to stand in for the self.

Foremost among these features would be the face. When you think about someone you know, you don't picture their toes; you picture their face. However, this only applies to other people. Your own face you cannot see; you can only see its reflection. Your eyes are part of your face, yet they can only look outward. They cannot look upon themselves. The aspect of the body with which we most closely identify is one we cannot see firsthand. This speaks to a powerful insight: the separated self can never see itself truly.

Look at yourself, and you will see a body. Look at this body in a different light and it looks different. And without a light it seems that it is gone. Yet you are reassured that it is there because you still can feel it with your hands and hear it move. Here is an image that you want to be yourself. It is the means to make your wish come true. It gives the eyes with which you look on it, the hands that feel it, and the ears with which you listen to the sounds it makes. It proves its own reality to you.

Thus is the body made a theory of yourself, with no provisions made for evidence beyond itself, and no escape within its sight.[3]

Further, we identify only the outer appearance of the body as *self*. No one puts framed photos from their colonoscopy up on the mantle or posts them to social media. The interior of the body strikes us as alien. It is so *not* "self" that it provokes a quiet embarrassment, disgust even, but not pride. Yet the body's interior is far more essential to preserving life than its outer appearance.

Back in medical school, as part of my psychiatry training, I read a book that served as an introduction to psychoanalytic theory and practice. One of its core teachings was that the ego begins as a body-based ego. Of course, the "ego" of psychoanalytic theory is not the same as the Course's ego, but it is nonetheless an attempt to understand how we develop a sense of self.

The physical body provides the foundation for our sense of self. It is with us from birth to death, our constant companion on this journey we call life. Even in dreams, we "see" and think in terms of bodies. It is very difficult to think of the self or others without picturing a body.

We could say that the body is the foundation upon which the false ego-self is constructed. How could the wholeness that is God and God's creation be viewed as separate unless there were some way to stand outside of it, look upon it, and judge it as something *other*, something different, something that is *not* self?

Of course, this is impossible. If you are an aspect of wholeness—if that is your true identity, your quintessential nature, what you were created to be—then you cannot change that. It lies beyond your power. A river cannot change its source or proclaim itself a desert or a mountain. But if that river were psychotic, it could claim to be whatever it wanted. Its water would still flow, it would still be a river, but it would no longer believe this of itself. Further, if it were able to hallucinate and actually see itself as a desert or mountain, that would be even more convincing—but only for itself. The rest of the world would not validate its delusional identity or share in its hallucination. The river might consider itself to be something it is not, but that in no way changes its reality.

This is the predicament in which we humans find ourselves. We have a body. It moves about in the world, it speaks to other bodies, it acquires its own personal history different from all others. (This means that no one can really understand it. It is unique in its loneliness—suffering quietly or loudly, along with everyone else.) It falls in and out of love. It joins with other bodies for a time, hoping to find a greater sense of purpose and meaning, but eventually it moves on, enticed by some other, still greater purpose. It is attacked by other bodies, but it can also be the attacker, always with some perfectly reasonable justification. ("They started it." "I was only acting in self-defense.")

The body is a tool of the ego, one that enables you to see yourself as separate and distinct: "I am me and you are not me." This is why the body is "the symbol of the ego." The body fulfills the ego's desire to be separate: separate from other bodies and separate from God. Without a body, how could the mind split itself and reinforce a sense of separation? This is achievable only through the body. But it comes at great cost. By investing belief in something that was not created and therefore does not truly exist, we lose sight of what we really are. *"Love, which created me, is what I am."*[4] We blind ourselves to this love. We slip into a dream in which we are no longer our true self. The river has convinced itself it is really a barren desert.

> *It is only the awareness of the body that makes love seem limited. For the body is a limit on love. The belief in limited love was its origin, and it was made to limit the unlimited. Think not that this is merely allegorical, for it was made to limit you. Can you who see yourself within a body know yourself as an idea? Everything you recognize you identify with externals, something outside itself. You cannot even think of God without a body, or in some form you think you recognize.*
>
> *The body cannot know. And while you limit your awareness to its tiny senses, you will not see the grandeur that surrounds you. God cannot come into a body, nor can you join Him there. Limits on love will always seem to shut Him out, and keep you apart from Him. The body is a tiny fence around a little part of a glorious and complete idea. It draws a circle, infinitely small, around a very little segment of Heaven, splintered from the whole, proclaiming that within it is your kingdom, where God can enter not.[5]*

Reading the Course's words, we may wonder why anyone would ever want to be such a thing as a body. What's the payoff in trying to limit Heaven and hold ourselves apart from the all-embracing love of God? It makes no sense, but that's what we've done. Take a look around at the ego's world—the rage, the competition, the bias—and it's pretty obvious that something has gone terribly wrong. The ego-self, enshrined in a body, is insane.

The trouble is, we've grown quite comfortable with insanity. We no longer recognize it as crazy. It has become the norm. We're in good company, though, because everybody is insane, so why bother trying to change? Besides, there are many tantalizing opportunities that the ego dangles before us that can only be achieved through the body. We chase one goal after another: success, fame, wealth, acclaim, sexual conquests. It's as if we were eating at what appeared to be a fine restaurant, managed by the ego as chef. The menu items sound amazing. And yet whatever we order, we somehow end up sick and still very hungry. At some point we must ask ourselves: How many dishes must we consume before we decide to stop eating at the ego's establishment and try someplace else? There must be a better source of nourishment.

The Ego's Monopoly Game

Imagine that you get together with your friends or family one relaxed evening for a fun game of Monopoly. First, you choose your playing pieces—because you can't play the game without a marker of some kind. There must be some representation of you, some symbol of *self* within the limited world of the game board, so you can participate. Your piece serves as a stand-in for your body. You recognize it as such. It is not really *you*, just a temporary representation of you that allows you to move around the board and play the game.

In the same way, you must have a body to "play" in the ego's world. There must be some central point from which your individual perception radiates outward. You see, hear, touch, smell, and taste the world around you. You learn to assemble these various perceptions into discrete people and events and then judge them as positive or negative according to your experience. You want more of the positive and less of the negative. In this way, you construct the parameters of the world you inhabit.

Here's the problem: everyone else is doing the same thing. And their perceptions and interpretations often differ from yours. We each arrive at our own version of "the truth." It requires little imagination to see how this situation can rapidly erupt into conflict. If your version of truth differs from mine, then one of us must be wrong. But it can't be me, so it must be you. My truth is true; yours is a lie. That makes you a liar. You are not like me. You are dangerous, untrustworthy, a threat. I will do my best to prove that you are wrong and lead you to the truth that I believe in.

We saw this play out in the U.S. presidential election of 2020, in which Donald Trump convinced tens of millions of his supporters that the election was rigged, even though he had zero proof and many down-ballot Republicans won their races. When there is no superordinate, objective truth—when our individual truths clash—the result is at best conflict; at worst, outright war.

This situation gives rise to what the Course calls the "first law of chaos": "*The truth is different for everyone.*"[6] Once this premise is accepted, chaos will inevitably follow.

Retuning to our Monopoly game and the choice of playing pieces, let's imagine that someone insists on being the dog; someone else likes the race car; another selects the hat. (No one wants to be the iron!) Even here, the ego's need for preference and specialness arises. Some pieces are more appealing than others, more special. I remember as a child fighting with my brother over who got to be the race car.

Then the game begins. You place your piece on the "Go" square along with the other players. You roll the dice and make your move. At first it's fun. You have plenty of money. You buy properties. You try to piece together a monopoly. Everyone laughs and enjoys themselves. But as the available properties dwindle and as houses and hotels spring up on your opponents' monopolies, the game takes on a darker cast. Each roll of the dice threatens you with potential bankruptcy.

Now let's imagine that something weird happens: a kind of "Freaky Friday" moment. By some strange enchantment, everyone forgets that it's just a game they're playing. The players *become* their playing pieces. They see only the game, only the board stretching out ahead of them, beckoning and threatening. With each roll of the die, each cycle around the board, the stakes grow higher. The pieces' fates are now determined by the spots on those two dice—where they land, whether they can pass safely or have to pay out and watch their funds evaporate. They can't stop playing. They can't just walk away from their reality. That's not an option. The idea would never occur to them, because *there is nothing else.* This game of Monopoly is all there is of life.

Now imagine that one of the other players awakens with a dim recollection that maybe Monopoly isn't all there is to life—that an entire rich world exists beyond the game. She tries to convince you and the others, but none of you care to listen. She's obviously nuts. When this "awakened one" finally gives up on all of you and quits the game, you shake your heads and mumble darkly among yourselves about how disturbed she is. "She just couldn't cut it. How sad that her life had to end that way. Whatever was she thinking? OK, whose turn is next?"

Obviously, this Monopoly game is another iteration of the virtual reality (VR) metaphor mentioned in the chapter on freedom. We are imprisoned in a VR construct (the Matrix). It is so compelling that it has become nearly impossible to escape from, precisely because we don't know we're in it! Our playing piece is our avatar, our symbolic body, and it has its own little adventure and life history. If it had only bought Boardwalk when it had the chance, it would own that monopoly. Instead, it's had the misfortune of landing on Boardwalk twice and paying outrageous rent to its owner.

Our lives are far more complex than a Monopoly game. The variety of goals and experiences available to us appears limitless. We want to give them all a try, if only we had enough years. The problem is that, even with limitless time, none of those goals or experiences will satisfy us. None will endure, because none are real. They are merely part of the dream of separation. You can't escape from a dream by dreaming about something else that's more interesting or less fearful. It's still a dream.

The Course reminds us that the body is *"the 'hero' of the dream"*:

The body is the central figure in the dreaming of the world. There is no dream without it, nor does it exist without the dream in which it acts as if it were a person to be seen and be believed. It takes the central place in every dream, which tells the story of how it was made by other bodies, born into the world outside the body, lives a little while and dies, to be united in the dust with other bodies dying like itself. In the brief time allotted it to live, it seeks for other bodies as its friends and enemies. Its safety is its main concern. Its comfort is its guiding rule. It tries to look for pleasure, and avoid the things that would be hurtful. Above all, it tries to teach itself its pains and joys are different and can be told apart.

The dreaming of the world takes many forms, because the body seeks in many ways to prove it is autonomous and real. It puts things on itself that it has bought with little metal discs or paper strips the world proclaims as valuable and real. It works to get them, doing senseless things, and tosses them away for senseless things it does not need and does not even want. It hires other bodies, that they may protect it and collect more senseless things that it can call its own. It looks about for special bodies that can share its dream. Sometimes it dreams it is a conqueror of bodies weaker than itself. But in some phases of the dream, it is the slave of bodies that would hurt and torture it.

The body's serial adventures, from the time of birth to dying, are the theme of every dream the world has ever had. The "hero" of this dream will never change, nor will its purpose.[7]

Reading these words, we recognize their truth, however reluctantly. But recognizing truth and living it are two different things. We do not want to give up what we think the body offers. We keep ordering more dishes from the ego's menu. But if we ever hope to awaken from this dream and free ourselves from the ego's Matrix world, we need to see its offerings for what they are: meaningless nothings, but in a form that makes them appear to glisten like priceless treasure. The belief that they have value keeps us enslaved to the ego and its proxy, the body. To divest from the body and its goals, we need to look at the underlying source of its appeal.

The Body's Treasures

A Course in Miracles tells us that "*The ego uses the body for attack, for pleasure and for pride.*"[8] Let's examine each of these in turn, because if we remain attached to even one tiny aspect, we will remain bound to the body and the ego.

ATTACK

The body allows us to take action and *do* things. With its hands we manipulate objects: lift and carry them, throw them, hide them. We can craft beautiful items like clothing, jewelry, and works of art, but we can also forge lethal weapons. With the body's mouth we learn to speak and communicate our wants and needs to others. We can kiss and sing, but also curse and scream. The body's legs let us move about. We are not plants; we are not confined to one place.

This would seem to be a good arrangement, until other bodies enter the picture. If you want to sit in a particular chair or play with a particular toy or object, but someone else wants the same thing, there is conflict. If you want to be first in line, but someone else elbows you out of the way, a fight could result. These situations arise frequently in childhood, and they're resolved by the adults in the room, because the adults are bigger, stronger, wiser, and better equipped to handle conflict. But what happens when the conflict is between two or more adults? What if those adults happen to own firearms? Who resolves things now? The police? The courts? Attorneys? An ambush in the dead of night? And what happens when the conflict is not among individuals, but nations? War becomes a real possibility.

The moment we view ourselves and others as bodies, we are separate. We perceive a gap between us and them. Furthermore, we don't know what that other body might be thinking or planning. What's their motivation? Are they a threat? Could they attack? Rob us? Rape us? Murder us? Should we take defensive action? Or maybe we should just attack them first in a preemptive strike.

With bodies, the threat of attack is ever present. In response, we buy weapons, train in martial arts, install alarm systems, carry pepper spray in our purses, fund police departments, maintain standing armies, engage in electronic surveillance. But do these measures really keep us safe? Or do they simply create more things to worry about, more things that could go wrong? They risk becoming like the finicky car alarm that sounds off whenever the wind gusts.

As I write this, the world remains in the midst of the coronavirus pandemic. This has exposed another, subtler, but perhaps even more daunting example of the vulnerability of bodies to attack. Not only do we not know what that other body might be thinking or plotting against us, but now, with the pandemic, they could be perfectly innocent, yet carrying a deadly disease. We can't tell. They can't either. Stand too close, and you risk catching it and spreading it. Unlike a direct attack, this threatens not only you, but everyone you come in contact with. Those you live with. Those you love. Contagion is another, covert form of attack that could not exist without the body.

To protect yourself, you keep your distance. To protect others, you wear a mask. These are sensible public health measures, of course, but we need to recognize how they reinforce the body's reality and the ever present threat of attack. As a body, you *are* vulnerable and in danger. Every time you venture outside your home or bring someone else into your home, you make a wager with illness and death.

I have been a student of *A Course in Miracles* for over forty-five years. You might think that by now I should be enlightened. (I've had the same thought myself many times!) Yet the temptation to attack remains an ingrained reflex. I very much want to see my brother's sinlessness: the goal of forgiveness. Yet when I walk along a deserted trail or a darkened city street and spy another person in the distance coming my way, my first thought is for my safety. Should I avoid eye contact? Or smile and stammer out a hello? Will they misinterpret my friendliness as an unwanted come-on? Or are they more likely to mug me?

As long as we identify with the body, attack will remain a powerful temptation, and one that's antithetical to peace.

PRIDE

Most of us cherish our bodies. What would we do without them? But inevitably, there is some feature we dislike and wish we could change. I recall a famous Hollywood star, a gorgeous woman, who in an interview admitted that she hated the way her lips curved: it reminded her of a duck's mouth. For others, it could be their noses or the way their hair curls. Plastic surgeons earn a fortune from such dislikes. Millions of books are sold every year that promise to reveal the secret of a new diet guaranteed to help you lose weight and look the way you've always wanted. And billions in profits are earned by the cosmetics industry to help adorn the body, cover up its blemishes and unpleasant smells, and accentuate its good features. If we're honest, we're all dissatisfied with our bodies to some degree. They fail our expectations in ways both subtle and glaring. In the worst case, these failures can pile up to the point where we come to hate our bodies.

Remember, the body is the symbol of the ego and therefore a visual, spatial representation of separation. There *is* a gap between us. We are different in appearance, and that difference extends to other aspects of our lives and personalities.

The ego thrives on the game of comparison, and the notion of separate bodies plays right into this proclivity. Differences give rise to judgments: one is "better," more desirable, while another is obviously inferior. Our focus drifts from forgiveness to manipulation and planning. How can we obtain the specialness that others have and we lack? We can emulate them, bond with them in a relationship, marry them, or murder them (and eliminate the threat to our egos). And yet, so long as we perceive a difference, we have bought into the idea of separation. It matters not which stratagem we employ to resolve the difference. It will fail. It must, because the idea of separation lies at its root. We can change the effect, but that is inconsequential as long as its cause remains unchanged.

At the other extreme, we feel pride in our bodies and their capabilities. We feel attractive and enjoy the attention that brings. We adorn the body with beautiful things like clothing and jewelry that display our fine aesthetic sense or signify our status in the world. (Why else would anyone pay such an exorbitant price for a Rolex watch?) We strut and preen and vamp. We feel good when other bodies are drawn to us and want to be close. But sometimes those other bodies want things from us in return that we don't care to give. At that point, things can get awkward, even violent.

If we have a particular talent or aptitude, we also feel pride. Whether with chess, athletics, or fashion, we enjoy competing with other bodies to see who "wins," who's "the best." The flip side is, however, that we can lose. We can compare and compete and still go away feeling nothing but shame.

Even if we do "win," how long do our victory and the resulting sense of pride endure? Only until the next opportunity for competition. It's a rare person who can win every time, everywhere. But win or lose, the outcome is never peace. We either have to defend our crown or slink away and find another arena in which to compete that suits us better.

In *From Loving One to One Love*, I wrote extensively about the nature of shame. Shame is barely mentioned in the Course: its sibling, guilt, gets the spotlight far more often. But like guilt, shame goes hand in hand with the ego. Both result from the core sense of lack that lies at the heart of the ego. How does the ego cope with this foundational sense of shame, this core stain that it can never sanitize or wash away? By attempting to cover it over and hide it behind a veneer of compensatory pride. "Pay no attention to my failures and losses. Look over here. See how well I've done in my career/investments/relationships!"

Shame and pride appear to be opposites. If I feel proud at my body's achievements, I can't simultaneously feel shame. But is this really so? The ego is a case study in shame, by definition. It is a nothingness parading as though it were everything. It cannot tolerate the idea of God, or of *you* as God created you, because that's a competition it knows it cannot win. It cares nothing for forgiveness. Why forgive the one who bested you? Instead, it prefers to divert attention elsewhere and keep us lurching from one goal to the next, playing its game in hopes that the next time, it will win! But if it does, it will need to win and win again to hold its shame at bay.

PLEASURE

Chapter 19 of the Course's Text enumerates four "obstacles to peace." The second of these is "*the belief the body is valuable for what it offers.*"[9] Of the body's many offerings, the most compelling is pleasure. Most of us do not relish attacking, and nobody wants to be attacked. Pride falls short and leaves us scrambling to recoup. But physical pleasure is different. It seems to be an inherent property of the body, much like its opposite, pain. No one wants pain, but humans will pay a great deal and willingly make sacrifices for a few moments of pleasure.

Think about the pleasures the body seems to offer. Food is high on the list. We have to eat to survive, and there is little stigma to enjoying good food. Cheeseburgers and fries, chocolate cake with ice cream, a gourmet meal with a fine Burgundy, or the refreshing chill of an ice-cold beer guzzled down on an unbearably hot day—they all have their appeal.

We enjoy other sensual pleasures as well: the scent of perfume or flowers, a beautiful sunset, a bracing massage, a magnificent work of art, a majestic symphony, your favorite band exploding into your favorite song as the crowd cheers and goes wild. The range of possible pleasures stretches from the quietly appealing to intensely exciting.

Many drugs induce pleasurable states. The mild lilting high from a few glasses of wine, the intense buzz of cocaine or meth, the bliss bath of intravenous heroin—these pleasures can be compelling, but they last only as long as the drug itself remains active in the body. To recapture the bliss, another dose of the drug becomes necessary. This sets up a cycle of addiction: craving, satisfaction, more craving.

I would venture, however, that the most compelling of the body's pleasures is sex. Throughout history, it has been the motivator behind a whole range of human behaviors, whether courting someone you're attracted to, taking secret time to pleasure yourself, or the raw hunger that drives some men to pay for sex with prostitutes. Sexual pleasure that culminates in orgasm is in itself a powerful drug. We want more. And like drugs, it can lead to life-crushing addiction.

What does the Course say about sex? On the surface, not a great deal. The word "sex" never appears in the edition authorized by its two scribes. In fact, it was present in the early Urtext (the original raw transcript of the Course), but only in relation to Bill and Helen's personal sexual issues. A remnant of this made it through to the current authorized edition, but the word "sexual" was replaced by "physical" at Helen Schucman's insistence.[10]

> *The confusion of miracle impulses with physical impulses is a major perceptual distortion. Physical impulses are misdirected miracle impulses. All real pleasure comes from doing God's Will.*[11]

The passage originally read, *"Sexual impulses are misdirected miracle impulses. All real pleasure comes from doing God's Will."* Sexuality pulls us toward union with each other. In that sense it is neither good nor bad. Union is the natural condition of our true Self; of course its appeal would filter into the ego's world of form. However, the pleasure arising from sexuality is as nothing compared to the pleasure of doing God's Will. We learn this not from books, but by putting it into practice.

The Course tells us many times that the key question to ask in any situation is "*What is it* for?"[12] What do you expect to come of it? What do you *want* to happen? And why? If we ask this about sexuality, we arrive at a number of different answers. At its most basic level, sex is about pleasure. It feels good. That makes it a very powerful reinforcer. Experiencing it, we want more. At the most abstract level, sex is for procreation. If you want a child, you will have to have intercourse (leaving aside artificial insemination). But I'd guess that fewer than a tenth of 1 percent of all sexual encounters have procreation as their goal. Quite the opposite. The so-called sexual revolution came into being only with the advent of accessible, reliable birth control.

But isn't sex an expression of love? It can be. Remember, we are laboring under the delusion that we are separate beings, even though in truth we are all one. At some deep level we retain an awareness of this. We are drawn to join with each other and unite, but mistaking ourselves for bodies, we attempt this union through the body. But the symbol of separation can never lead to union, and after sex, our individual identities reassert themselves. This helps to explain the awkward silence and paradoxical sense of distance that often follows sex. We joined together; it was intimate and intense, but unsustainable. Now, back in our separate selves, the sense of isolation is all the more pronounced as a result of the contrast.

According to the Course, minds are capable of joining. (Indeed, they *must* join if they are to awaken.) Bodies are not. The union of sexual intercourse and the bliss of orgasm fade rapidly, leaving us once again with our individual lives and problems.

The attempt to achieve union through sex, through the body, illustrates the Course's point that bodies are incapable of true joining. The body is the symbol of the ego and the literal embodiment of separation. How could it merge with another body, also a symbol of separation, to form a whole? Interpenetration is not oneness.

The all-encompassing bliss of a powerful orgasm which wipes away awareness of all else comes very close to the experience of mystical union. But once again, *it does not last*. The Course tells us in Workbook lesson 133, "*I will not value what is valueless*": if you cherish something, but it doesn't last—that is, if it's not eternal—then it isn't truly valuable. Not in the eyes of the Holy Spirit. Everything created by God is eternal; everything else is illusion and delusion— nothingness in the form of something and therefore of no value whatsoever. To pursue it is futile, a waste of time.

If we accept that the attempt to unite with others through the body is meaningless because it cannot result in true union, does that then mean we should swear off having sex? Take vows of celibacy? It could be argued that if it feels good—if it makes you happy—then what's the problem? The Course tells us that there is a problem: pleasure derived from the body ratifies the body's reality for us. If we pursue pleasure and thereby make the body real—if we accept that this symbol of separation is capable of bringing joy to the Son of God—then we must *be* our bodies. Such a belief represents a step backward from what the Course attempts to teach.

More worrisome still, if we pursue pleasure through the body, we open ourselves to pleasure's flip side: pain. If the body can bring pleasure, it can also bring its opposite, pain.

> *It is impossible to seek for pleasure through the body and not find pain. It is essential that this relationship be understood, for it is one the ego sees as proof of sin. It is not really punitive at all. It is but the inevitable result of equating yourself with the body, which is the invitation to pain.*[13]

Anything that strengthens your identification with the body will leave you more susceptible to pain. Understanding this, you'd think that every student of *A Course in Miracles* would give up sex. But that's not necessarily a useful goal. If you crave sex, but in your embarrassment force yourself to give it up, it still remains valuable in your mind. You cannot avoid feeling you've made a sacrifice. You might construe it as a noble sacrifice, but the Course does not ask sacrifice of you or anyone. Jesus makes this very clear in chapter 6 of the Text. His crucifixion was not a sacrifice; rather, it was a demonstration of the body's impermanence and lack of value. Sacrifice implies loss—a willful surrender of something you still desire in order to achieve a higher goal. But this runs contrary to the very first principle of miracles:

> *There is no order of difficulty in miracles. One is not harder or bigger than another. They are all the same. All expressions of love are maximal.*[14]

There is no order of difficulty in miracles because there is no hierarchy of illusions. No illusion is more or less real than any other. They are all equally *unreal*. That is why miracles apply equally to everyone in this VR Matrix world. If you give up one form of illusion only to embrace another, you have not awakened. You remain dreaming.

Furthermore, if you believed that you had to give up sex to avoid pleasure and pain, wouldn't you logically need to extend this to all other activities that give rise to some form of sensual pleasure? No more fine food or wine. No singing or dancing to music. No massages. No yoga. If you behold a resplendent sunset, must you shut your eyes and pretend it out of existence so as not to be tempted by the ego?

These experiences are all equally unreal, so it could be argued that they should be shunned to avoid any deepening of our identification with the body. But is this practical? Is it effective? Is this what the Course asks of us? Because beauty can also be transformative, as I discussed in chapter 3 of *From Never-Mind to Ever-Mind*.

It seems very pat to state that nothing in this world is real, including the body, and therefore to give it any kind of attention is to feed the ego. After all, the separation never occurred in God's reality; we remain at one with God. So there's nothing we need to do here in the world to awaken. There's nothing we *can* do. Reality will prevail. It's only a matter of time. Our role is to shorten that time by identifying and "*removing the blocks [in our minds] to the awareness of love's presence.*"[15]

The attempt to deny the body paradoxically establishes a false dualism. Yes, we remain as God created us. Yes, the material world, the world we project outside ourselves in a futile attempt to offload our guilt and shame, *is* illusion. But if you are reading this, if you are breathing, *you are still here, still living in that world*! The nondual universe of God and God's creations is unaffected by our delusional separation, but that's not where the problem lies. That's not where the work needs to be done. To shun the world we're living in because in an absolute sense it is unreal is not what the Holy Spirit asks of us.

The Course is very clear that our task is to bring our illusions to the truth, and not the other way around. You can't bring truth into the world of illusion to somehow sanctify the body and make it holy. Truth brought to illusion is no longer truth; it becomes another aspect of the dream. Our task, with the Holy Spirit as guide and coach, is to uncover all of those preferences and habits that keep us attached to the world . . . and then, when we're finally ready, to let them go. As we said earlier, this usually takes time. The Holy Spirit reveals them to us according to our level of readiness. We can choose to close our eyes and proclaim that truth is already here, and, although this is true in the ultimate sense, it is unlikely to help you the next time your partner or your kids trigger you into anger.

The Course does not prescribe asceticism in any form. Quite the contrary: to spurn an activity with prejudice is to invest it with meaning. Forgiveness does just the opposite. It gently demonstrates that there is no meaning in illusions. They offer no path to lasting happiness and so we should *want* to be free of them. We learn to set aside our need to plan and control. Instead, we open our minds to the Holy Spirit's judgment, substituting His for ours.

While we are here in the world, believing we are a body, we will still have needs and cravings. We need to breathe, eat, urinate, sleep, and so on. These are not inherently bad. Nor are they good. They are simply aspects of life as a separated being. You can try to swear off breathing, eating, sleeping—but to what end? Death is not enlightenment!

At some point we will no longer be enslaved to the body's needs. But the timing is not up to us. I am frequently asked by Course students, "How can I awaken faster?" "Can you give me any tips for letting go of this or that problem? Chronic pain? Alcoholism? Cancer? An addictive relationship?" I remind those who ask such questions that "faster" and "slower" are relative terms; they only make sense within the world of time. They require us to make a judgment, an assessment about our progress: how long something actually takes to happen, in contrast to our expectations about how long it should take. In eternity, where time does not exist, "faster" and "slower" have no meaning.

Eternity is the goal. From the perspective of eternity, it doesn't matter whether you needed two minutes or two millennia to awaken. Remember, we never separated from God in the first place. Therefore, even the idea of awakening remains part of the dream: a constructive part—in fact, the only goal worth pursuing here—but still falling short of eternity. Like all things in the curriculum of the Atonement, we leave the pace of learning to the Holy Spirit, who knows far better than we do our readiness for each step. Awakening cannot be compelled.

I once worked in psychotherapy with a man, a Course student, who was addicted to pornography. On his thirteenth birthday, his father had bought him a subscription to *Playboy*. I suspect he was trying to fulfill his role as a dad and explain sexuality to his son without risking his own personal embarrassment. This was in the days before the Internet made porn ubiquitous. There were few other ways to see naked women. My patient was delighted, of course.

Whatever his intentions, this man's father planted the seeds for an almost fifty-year struggle with pornography and sexual addiction. My patient would page through his *Playboy* collection searching out the photos he found most stimulating. He'd masturbate, feel guilty, and swear off porn. He'd throw out a magazine or two as a token of his newfound conviction, experiencing a wave of relief. But in a matter of days, if not hours, he'd be back to viewing his favorite nudes.

He graduated from *Playboy* to *Penthouse*, just as any addict will gravitate toward stronger drugs. In those days, every convenience store sold the magazines, so every trip to buy a can of soda became a struggle with temptation. At one point, in a fit of shame and guilt, he tossed his entire magazine collection in the trash. It felt like an incredible achievement—and a terrible sacrifice. Within a week, one of his dorm mates returned from a visit to his grandparents with ten years of *Playboy* crated in boxes. His grandparents were moving and didn't want to bring them along. His dorm mate didn't want them either, so he passed them along to my patient. Just like that, he was struggling once again with his porn addiction.

This man's first two marriages scored no prizes for sexual chemistry. He felt frustrated and turned to his reliable fallback: porn. By contrast, he and his third wife shared outstanding sexual chemistry. And yet the lure of the magazines remained strong. He'd stash them in inconvenient places like the back of the garage, hoping this would deter him. It did not. He struck all kinds of bargains with himself about what he'd allow into the house. For perhaps ten years, this uneven truce held sway.

Then something happened that was out of his control. His wife got sick. She grew so ill, so frail, that even the thought of sex was out of the question. She saw a doctor, got tests, and was diagnosed with cancer. He retreated to his porn collection (at this point all online; no more magazines). However, looking at his wife, seeing her pain, her fragility, her weight loss, he came to a decision. He could no longer indulge his addictive sexual cravings. Lusting after young porn models may not constitute an affair, but it was still a betrayal of his wife. With this insight, he found he no longer wanted to engage with the seductive images on his computer monitor. The appeal was no longer there. He deleted his entire online collection. Nor did he backslide when, six months later, his wife was pronounced cured. He was finished with porn—not because he'd sworn off of it or forced himself into a grand sacrifice. It was simply, finally, the right time and the right thing for him to do. He was ready. He felt much gratitude for how Spirit had brought this about.

I share this man's story to illustrate how the Holy Spirit works with us, at our own pace. Miracles, like forgiveness, come only when we are truly ready. No doubt there are some who in a flash of epiphany walk away from their addictions and never look back. But I suspect that for each one of those, there are thousands more like my patient, who are enslaved to some addictive body-centered pleasure and see no way out.

Patience is one of the key characteristics of a teacher of God. Because time is simply another aspect of the ego's illusion, some things will appear to take time to work out. The Course tells us, *"Fear not that you will be abruptly lifted up and hurled into reality. Time is kind, and if you use it on behalf of reality, it will keep gentle pace with you in your transition."*[16] We don't know the way to return to God. We are too lost in dreaming. We need a guide. Nor are we in charge of the timing. For these, we need the Holy Spirit. It's His function to take everything we made in support of separation and repurpose it for communication and joining. We don't even recognize most of our deeper egoic programming. We cannot see it until we're ready. We tackle one set of attachments, congratulate ourselves on how well we're doing, and then discover the next layer. It lay hidden until we cleared the layers above it. Our issues arise and peel away like the skins of an onion.

Would my patient have chosen that his wife get cancer? Of course not. Yet her diagnosis brought them both, each in their own way, into greater awareness of the need for changes that could not otherwise have been achieved. Therefore, I was only momentarily surprised when this man shared with me that he considered his wife's cancer a miracle. Having fulfilled its function, it was no longer needed.

Practice

Take a moment to review the past few days of your life. Which of the body's "gifts" have you valued? Which did you chase after?

- Where did you take joy in a display of power? (For parents, think about your children!)
- Were there any situations in which you felt proud of yourself? If so, when? And why? What led to the feeling? Did that pride come at the expense of another?
- Were there people, bodies, that you found sexually attractive? Colleagues? Parents of your kids' friends? Actors on television or Facebook?
- What actions did you take to look and feel more attractive? How much time and effort went into the outfit you're wearing? Or that you wore over the weekend? Did you put on makeup? Groom your hair? Why or why not?
- Whom did you attack and who appeared to attack you? Remember, attack isn't necessarily a physical assault. A nasty remark, a dirty look, a sarcastic quip, being a bit too rough—all will suffice.
- How has your body brought you pleasure in the past few days? Were there meals, snacks, or desserts that you enjoyed? Were there any you craved? Did you masturbate? If so, what was the impetus?
- Did you take any drugs? A glass of wine, a shot of whiskey? A quick hit on the vape?

Now step back and consider all of the ways you allowed your body to rule your life over these few days, prioritizing its needs and desires. Just notice it. No guilt, shame, or recrimination necessary. We cannot change until we make ourselves aware of just how much of a prisoner to the ego we are.

"Gifts" of the Body, Part Two

Having taken that brief tour of your body's "gifts," let's now also acknowledge another set of "gifts" that come to us through the body. These are darker. We do not seek them out; we do our best to avoid them. But they are the inevitable results of feeling and behaving as if the body were our true self.

PAIN

A Course in Miracles tells us that pain and pleasure are essentially the same. This does not make sense until you understand that, from the Course's perspective, they are the same *because they share the same purpose.* They validate the body's reality and the idea that it can provide something of value. But if the body can bring pleasure, it can bring pain as well.

It's interesting to consider the ratio of pain to pleasure that we experience over a lifetime. During infancy, the ratio is quite high, as pain and suffering far outweigh pleasure. Pain is there from the start, beginning at birth and continuing with hunger, skin rashes, poor digestion, inconsistent sleep, accidents and, in some families, harsh discipline. This persists more or less until a child is capable of getting most of her needs fulfilled, whether by herself or by asking others for help.

The pain-pleasure ratio hits its lowest point in young adulthood, when our bodies tend to be robust and healthy and we think we know who we are, what we want, and how to go about getting it. If I think back to my twenties and thirties, I recollect more opportunities for pleasure than pain. (We are only talking about bodily pleasure and pain here, not emotional. That would tip the balance considerably in the other direction.)

As we age, the pain-pleasure ratio increases markedly. We injure ourselves. We develop bodily afflictions that don't heal fully, chronic conditions that continue to dog us throughout our life. We try to fend these off through a host of healthy practices: good nutrition, regular doctor's visits, herbal supplements, daily exercise routines. But at some point, our efforts begin to fall short. Back pain or shin splints prevent us from exercising. Genetics assert themselves: a forcible reminder that we cannot escape our parents' destinies.

Then there is the inevitable war of attrition that is aging. The body can no longer do the things it once did. Its strength diminishes. Its memory frays. No wonder we eventually need to retire. We can't keep running with the young bulls; we can't keep up. Illnesses become more frequent and more severe. As we age, health preoccupies us, to the exclusion of other activities.

How do we react to aging? Many try to deny it. They stay current with the latest fashions. They continue to play sports and drive sports cars. They have affairs. They get plastic surgery. They travel. However, none of these can halt the inevitable, inexorable incursion of old age. In our society, we don't care to witness aging. We hide the geriatric population in nursing homes. We can visit, but we can also leave at any time we choose.

In other societies, aging is not a curse to be avoided, but a marker of wisdom and value. The elders are consulted about problems and their opinions valued. The condition of their physical bodies is irrelevant to their accumulated wisdom. This attitude is helpful both for the elders and the young. All are valued and integral to a whole, healthy community.

ILLNESS

Everyone has experienced illness at some time. Most illnesses are short-lived and inconvenient, but not life-threatening. A runny nose and scratchy throat may make you miserable for a day or two, but will not kill you.

The first experience of illness usually comes in childhood. You run a fever. You ache all over. You vomit. In a psychologically healthy family, you're supported and cared for. In a dysfunctional family, you may be neglected or even punished for your infirmity. Either way, you learn that the body can cause suffering.

For some, the role of sickness grows appealing. You snuggle in bed while your mother brings you soup, toast, and tea. Maybe she sits with you and reads, or sings, or tells stories. Being sick might be the only time you receive loving attention from your parents. In such instances, the sick role can become desirable. With serious or chronic disease, sickness becomes part of your self-image, granting you certain privileges, but also limiting your activities in important ways.

For many, however, illness is a curse, an impediment. It blocks you from activities you enjoy. You can't go outside and play with your friends. You're forced to miss the big game, the office party, or the school dance.

Robust health and physical ability can also become part of the self-image, especially during the school years, when sports play such a big role in determining social circles. There is a world of difference between being picked first for the baseball team and being the last, wanted by no one.

At some point, people we know and love get sick. Some die, never to be seen again. Our reactions depend on our past experience, our ability to understand what's happened, and our support and coping systems. We can react with denial—"that will never happen to me"—or over-concern—"I will start jogging and take vitamins to protect myself." Eventually, we resume life as usual. But behind the normalcy lurks a sense of the body's frailty and impermanence.

Illness can be scary. Before the advent of modern medicine, any bout with sickness could potentially kill you. Today, we have less fear. We trust that whatever afflicts us will pass or be cured by our doctors. But the fear shows up when the illness is one that medicine has no remedy for, like certain cancers. In those instances, life's uncertainty and the fear of death never fully recede. They become constant companions.

Fear of illness ultimately leads to fear of death. Most of us barely give death a thought in our day-to-day lives: we push it away to focus on more immediate concerns, like paying the bills or preparing dinner. But every adult knows that at some future point, their life will come to an end. They will die. So will everyone they know. This makes the future a scary place.

We try to insulate ourselves from the fear of certain death. We console ourselves that our memory will live on through our children. We buy life insurance to ensure that those we love will have enough money to survive without us. Some hope to live on through their achievements, whether building a thriving business or writing a great novel. But no achievement can forestall death.

The Course tells us that death is the ego's friend because it "proves" that we are vulnerable and mortal. In the ego's mind, death challenges the very idea of an eternal, loving God. How could such a God possibly exist if we are all doomed to die? How could a loving God allow this? He could not, and therefore God does not exist.

Therefore, as much as we might fear death, at a deep, unconscious level we actually believe that we deserve death as the penalty for separating from God. Our guilt demands it. It remains attractive and preferable to the wrath of an angry, vengeful deity, or to continuing to wrestle with life's blows and insults. Death is the ultimate avoidance mechanism, the exit ramp from whatever problems we face and cannot seem to solve.

The Course offers a very different understanding of sickness. Workbook lesson 136 states that "*Sickness is a defense against the truth.*" Sickness "proves" that we hostage to the body (and of course the ego), that we are weak and powerless, but most of all, that we are separate individuals battling it out on our own. "*All sickness comes from separa-*

tion."[17] If I am ill and you are not, then obviously we are different. You may feel compassion for me, you may even want to help me, but my illness sets me apart from you. I am sick, while you are healthy. By reinforcing this sense of separation and difference, sickness pushes truth away. It defends us against what we fear to look upon, much less embrace, that is, our true identity in God, as love, our innocence from sin, and the recognition that our brothers are one with us.

> *All forms of sickness, even unto death, are physical expressions of the fear of awakening.*[18]

> *How do you think that sickness can succeed in shielding you from truth? Because it proves the body is not separate from you, and so you must be separate from the truth. You suffer pain because the body does, and in this pain are you made one with it. Thus is your "true" identity preserved, and the strange, haunting thought that you might be something beyond this little pile of dust silenced and stilled. For see, this dust can make you suffer, twist your limbs and stop your heart, commanding you to die and cease to be.*
> *Thus is the body stronger than the truth, which asks you live, but cannot overcome your choice to die.*[19]

When we feel sick, we do feel hostage to the body. It is hard to focus on other goals or activities. We withdraw. We look to other people for help, but we keep our expectations in check. We resort to what the Course calls "magic" to heal us. The word "magic" refers any intervention that seems to come from outside ourselves, whether medication, surgery, nutritional supplements, exercise, chiropractic, yoga—and the list goes on. By investing belief in such magical solutions, we can and do recover from illness. But at the cost of forgetting our true nature.

There are two problems with relying on magic. First, it does not address the problem at its source, which is the mind. We wind up in a noxious game of whack-a-mole in which we alleviate one symptom, only to have a different problem spring up elsewhere in the body or in our lives. Magic does not heal; it postpones and cloaks the need for the decision to truly heal, because it does nothing to remedy the source of illness, which lies in the desire of the split mind to be separate.

Second, we do not feel empowered by magic solutions. We attribute our cure to some agent outside of and apart from ourselves. We are at the receiving end of the illness and also the cure. Both exist independently out there in the world and therefore beyond our ability to perfectly control. This arrangement offers no certainty and little trust. We remain insecure. Illness could return, or another could arise at any time. We do our best not to think about this and carry on, but like a lurking shadow, fear huddles ever present in the darker corners of our mind.

By contrast, *A Course in Miracles* is clear that the source of all illness lies in the mind, and therefore a true cure can come only from the mind.

The acceptance of sickness as a decision of the mind, for a purpose for which it would use the body, is the basis of heal-

ing. And this is so for healing in all forms. A patient decides that this is so, and he recovers. If he decides against recovery, he will not be healed. Who is the physician? Only the mind of the patient himself. The outcome is what he decides that it is. Special agents seem to be ministering to him, yet they but give form to his own choice. He chooses them in order to bring tangible form to his desires. And it is this they do, and nothing else. They are not actually needed at all. The patient could merely rise up without their aid and say, "I have no use for this." There is no form of sickness that would not be cured at once.

What is the single requisite for this shift in perception? It is simply this: the recognition that sickness is of the mind, and has nothing to do with the body.[20]

If this is the first time you've encountered the idea that the mind is the primary source of everything we perceive in the world, it may well seem radical or insane. We resist such a disruptive idea because it would compel us to revise all we think we know about the world. We'd rather cling to the familiar beliefs we've always lived by. But ask yourself if the status quo is really working for you. How healthy do you feel? How often do you awaken looking forward to the day ahead? How often do you experience true joy unrelated to anything outside yourself?

Then go further. Consider the world we inhabit. Watch or read the news. Violence and prejudice are everywhere. According to the zero-sum thinking that the world subscribes to—"what I gain, you lose; what you get somehow comes at my expense"—competition is natural, essential for survival. But no matter how much you or anyone else happens to gain, no matter who appears to win, at the end death awaits us all.

Are we pleased with this situation? Recall that the impetus for the Course was Bill Thetford's impassioned plea to Helen Schucman that "there must be a better way" to deal with their toxic work environment. The Course is an instruction manual for finding that "better way." If we put its ideas into practice, we will have little to lose and much to be gained.

*   *   *

How does the Course see the body? Obviously not for strengthening the separation. What, then, is its purpose when we relinquish ego goals and put the Holy Spirit in charge? Recall that the Holy Spirit's function is to reinterpret everything that we've used for separation, competition, and attack. He uses these to promote forgiveness and lead us to our true identity in wholeness and peace. In our separated state, it is difficult to imagine what this is like.

> *Christ's vision has one law. It does not look upon a body, and mistake it for the Son whom God created. It beholds a light beyond the body; an idea beyond what can be touched. . . . It sees no separation. And it looks on everyone, on every circumstance, all happenings and all events, without the slightest fading of the light it sees.*[21]

The Holy Spirit has only one purpose for the body: as a communication device. We believe we are separate. We believe we are our bodies. How can we move toward the union and oneness that is the true nature of the Son of God unless those bodies learn to communicate love instead of fear and strife? As we let go of our grievances against others, truth has a chance to enter. We see our brothers and sisters not as threats or purveyors of specialness, but as the holy Son of God. As we embrace this understanding, we begin to experience the same thing in ourselves. This is the process that the Course calls forgiveness, and it was the subject of the second half of *From Loving One to One Love*. What we see in others we reinforce for ourselves.

> *The body is beautiful or ugly, peaceful or savage, helpful or harmful, according to the use to which it is put.*[22]

> *If you use the body for attack, it is harmful to you. If you use it only to reach the minds of those who believe they are bodies, and teach them through the body that this is not so, you will understand the power of the mind that is in you.*[23]

Communication does not mean verbal communication exclusively. You do not have to travel the world preaching the Couse to everyone you meet. Should you find yourself in conversation with someone who is curious about the Course, please do discuss it. But the Course is clear that we are all students *and* teachers. We teach by how we live. We demonstrate peace or attack. If we hold a calm, quiet center within, despite the turmoil surrounding us; if we respond internally, in our thoughts, with love, even to those who trigger us; we are teaching peace.

Recall that "the sole responsibility of the miracle worker is to accept the Atonement for himself."[24] The only mind over which you have direct influence is your own. *I rule my mind, which I alone must rule.*[25] However, mind is not individualized or private, except to the ego. Your mind is interconnected with all others, because in truth there is only one Mind: that of God and His Son, in Whom we all have our being. If we are to mend the separate pieces of self and bind them together again in wholeness as God created them, we must start by healing our own misperceptions. In the hands of the Holy Spirit, this generalizes to other minds that believe they are isolated and private, and calling out for help and healing. In this way, "*an interlocking chain of forgiveness*" is forged, "*which, when completed, is the Atonement.*"[26]

The Holy Spirit enables us to overlook the body and all other obstacles to peace, weakening the boundaries that maintain the illusion of separation. Minds begin to recall their unity. You might think of your mind (and others) as a hologram that can stand on its own within the illusion, but which also encompasses all Mind, all reality. You teach peace and love by practicing peace and love. Make these the centerpiece of your own being, and your brothers and sisters will inevitably benefit.

The power of one mind can shine into another, because all the lamps of God were lit by the same spark. It is everywhere and it is eternal.[27]

No thought of God's Son can be separate or isolated in its effects. Every decision is made for the whole Sonship, directed in and out, and influencing a constellation larger than anything you ever dreamed of.[28]

Communication joins us together. We share the learning. All other uses of the body reinforce separation and keep us apart. Illness is one result of this separation. Ideally, then, to heal illness we must address its source in the separation. To the extent that we are able to commit our thoughts to this purpose, we allow healing. *"Healing is the result of using the body solely for communication."*[29] *"Health is the result of relinquishing all attempts to use the body lovelessly."*[30]

This understanding opens an entirely new perspective on illness and how to resolve it. Like all things we give to the Holy Spirit, illness becomes an opportunity to forgive—ourselves and others. We must look within and discover those times when we responded to a brother with anything other than love. We unearth our own deepseated sense of guilt and inadequacy and release this to the Holy Spirit. Will this result in an instant cure? It might, but not necessarily. If the sudden disappearance of symptoms would prove too disruptive to your belief system, if it would leave you fearful, then a gradual lifting of symptoms will prove more productive. You are better off if you refrain from judgments about your condition or your progress. But even if your symptoms appear unaffected, you will experience more peace. You will benefit, as will those around you.

It seems to be the body that we feel limits our freedom, makes us suffer, and at last puts out our life. Yet bodies are but symbols for a concrete form of fear. Fear without symbols

*calls for no response, for symbols can stand for the meaning-
less. Love needs no symbols, being true. But fear attaches to
specifics, being false.*[31]

Bodies attack, but minds do not.[32]

Practice
Catalog all your body's ills and hurts. Do they contrast
with or confirm your self-image?

4

The Separation

Almost everyone knows the story of Adam and Eve from the Bible. Here's a quick summary. Adam and Eve live in happy innocence in the Garden of Eden, free to do whatever they please except that they must not eat from one particular tree: the tree of knowledge of good and evil. God has forbidden this. However, the serpent tempts Eve to eat the fruit. She in turn convinces Adam to do the same. In an instant, their innocence is lost. Embarrassed by what they've done, and ashamed over discovering they are naked, they try to hide from God. For their disobedience, He banishes them from Eden and sends them out into the cold world, where food is scarce and hardly guaranteed.

In the Judeo-Christian tradition, this event is known as the Fall. The conventional Christian notion of original sin is traced back to Eve and Adam's defiance of God. We are all sinners, all fallen, because of their disobedience. That is their legacy to us.

A Course in Miracles addresses the Fall only briefly, in the early chapters of the Text. It sees the Fall as an analogue or symbol of the separation from God, which gave rise to the ego and to the world as we know it. *"Until the 'separation,' which is the meaning of the 'fall,' nothing was lacking. There were no needs at all. Needs arise only when you deprive yourself."*[1]

The separation took us from a state of absolute wholeness and completion, where nothing was lacking (nor could ever be lacking), and plunged us into a world where lack is a given. Almost all of us feel that we are lacking something, whether an object, an ability, recognition, or love itself. In the separated state, we no longer acknowledge our intimate relationship with God, our Creator. We believe we have become something other than His Son. We identify with the ego and embrace its false, limited sense of self. As a result, we feel alone, different from others, captive to a physical body which is vulnerable to illness and injury and must ultimately die. We are left to fend for ourselves in an uncertain world. This cannot help but produce fear.

Of course, God did not create the separation, so by definition it is unreal: the only reality is God and His creations. The separation occurred only in the mind of the Son. We do not have the capacity to change the nature of our true Self. We cannot undo God's Will. But because we believe in the separation—we made it happen, after all—it seems all too real for us.

The separation is a system of thought real enough in time, though not in eternity. All beliefs are real to the believer.

The fruit of only one tree was "forbidden" in the symbolic garden. But God could not have forbidden it, or it could not have been eaten. If God knows His children, and I assure you that He does, would He have put them in a position where their own destruction was possible? The "forbidden tree" was named the "tree of knowledge." Yet God created knowledge and gave it freely to His creations. The symbolism here has been given many interpretations, but you may be sure that any interpretation that sees either God or His creations as capable of destroying Their Own purpose is in error.

Eating of the fruit of the tree of knowledge is a symbolic expression for usurping the ability for self-creating.[2]

The Course defines the word "knowledge" as that which comes only from God. It is not content, not a collection of facts, but rather a state of all-inclusive beingness. Here on earth we do not have knowledge in this sense. Instead we have perception, which leads to belief in a world of illusion. (We'll look at this in more depth in the following chapter.) We bartered knowledge, along with the awareness of our true Self, for an illusion of specialness. We wanted to be unique. Even love as we experience it here is predicated on specialness. The partner we desire is someone with special qualities which we admire and feel we lack. We seek to appropriate their specialness by falling in love with them, wooing them and tying them, along with their special qualities, to us for life. If you've lived long enough, you know how that works out!

Eating the forbidden fruit of the tree of knowledge is a symbolic depiction of the separation from God. It did not lead us to knowledge, however, for that we already had. On the contrary, it cloaked knowledge and brought us delusion, insanity, and suffering. *"The world began with one strange lesson, powerful enough to render God forgotten, and His Son an alien to himself, in exile from the home where God Himself established him."*[3]

After eating the forbidden fruit, Adam and Eve become aware of good and evil. They have entered a world of opposites and contrast—a world of duality. Duality shatters oneness; the two cannot coexist. God does not know duality. How could He? God's nature is wholeness and love. It has no parts, no divisions. With the separation we have declared that we are unlike God and in opposition to His Kingdom. At best, we play the role of the tragic hero, persevering as best we can in a cruel and difficult world that is destined one day to kill us. At worst, we feel totally helpless, at the whim of forces beyond our control. This is frightening. We make plans that cannot satisfy for long. We fall into despair, and still we die. "There must be a better way."

Dissociation and Separation

A Course in Miracles was scribed in the 1960s and early '70s by a collaboration between two highly respected academic psychologists. They were well versed in psychoanalytic theory and practice. As a result, ideas like defense mechanisms are prominent throughout the Course. Many feel that the Course could not have been written, much less received, without this foundation in psychological theory.

Two defenses, dissociation and projection, are central to any understanding of the separation and how it is maintained. *"Exclusion and separation are synonymous, as are separation and dissociation. We have said before that the separation was and is dissociation, and that once it occurs projection becomes its main defense, or the device that keeps it going."*[4] Unfortunately, most people have little understanding of these defense mechanisms and how they operate. Even psychologists will often misconstrue the mechanics of dissociation. Yet they are key to understanding the separation and what's required to reverse it.

What is dissociation?

Dissociation is a distorted process of thinking whereby two systems of belief which cannot coexist are both maintained. If they are brought together, their joint acceptance becomes impossible. But if one is kept in darkness from the other, their separation seems to keep them both alive and equal in their reality. Their joining thus becomes the source of fear, for if they meet, acceptance must be withdrawn from one of them. You cannot have them both, for each denies the other.[5]

We have all used dissociation. In *From Never-Mind to Ever-Mind*, I gave the example of an experiment in which a subject is hypnotized (hypnotic trance is a dissociative state) and pain is inflicted on her arm. The subject is told that she feels no pain, and indeed, she sits comfortably, showing no signs of distress. She's then told that one of her arms can feel pain and can write about its experience. That arm howls in pain, in writing, while the subject continues to sit placidly.

The arm, along with the pain, is dissociated from the mainstream of consciousness. This can be helpful and adaptive if there are no other options for managing the pain. But it can also be destructive. If you are unaware of pain, you will do nothing to relieve it and damage can result.

This is a relatively simple example of dissociation in a controlled setting. Let's look at more extreme example of dissociation, that of dissociative identity disorder (DID), or as it's more commonly known, multiple personality. (I devoted a chapter to this subject in *From Never-Mind to Ever-Mind*.) Individuals afflicted with this condition display two or more alternate personas (or "alters"). They can have different genders, ages, names, body types, and handedness, as well as different skills. One might be a painter or pianist, while others have no such abilities. Alters usually have very different, even opposing, personalities. Some are brash and aggressive, others meek and conciliatory. There are documented cases of alters with allergies or medical conditions like diabetes that vanish when a different alter takes charge.

Each alter has its own set of memories as well. Some memories are accessible to other alters while others remain intensely personal and closely hidden. Alters can eavesdrop on each other. One can influence the behavior of another who is out in the world, often without that alter knowing why they're acting the way they are. Clearly, this condition does not make for an easy life.

In DID, the alters are all copresent in the mind but kept separate by dissociation. There is no conscious ability to switch from one to the other on demand. (With treatment, they can be taught this skill.) In a sense, each has its own inner and outer life more or less related to what the others may be experiencing. Their inner lives can be quite rich and detailed, with entire landscapes in which they play, sleep, and hang out. A child alter, for instance, might frequent a playground with a swing set. Alters are very protective of their identities. They do not give them up easily, even when faced with the devastation caused by their condition. They fear the loss of their sense of self, just as we all do when faced with the truth of our Identity in God. And yet to reawaken to knowledge and to God is inevitable, because that is our Identity. There is nothing fearful about truth. The fear comes from not knowing what you are.

> *Unless you first know something you cannot dissociate it. Knowledge must precede dissociation, so that dissociation is nothing more than a decision to forget. What has been forgotten then appears to be fearful, but only because the dissociation is an attack on truth. You are fearful because you have forgotten. And you have replaced your knowledge by an awareness of dreams because you are afraid of your dissociation, not of what you have dissociated. When what you have dissociated is accepted, it ceases to be fearful.*[6]

What is the cause of DID? What would lead the mind to fracture in this way? Severe, repeated early childhood trauma and abuse. A very young child lacks the capacity to cope with physical and/or sexual abuse inflicted by an adult they would otherwise be expected to trust. They can't understand it, nor do they have the internal fortitude to report it to a parent or authority figure. Even when they do, they're often disbelieved, accused of lying, and punished.

As a result, these children cope internally by dissociating the abuse. Now it didn't happen to them, but to that *other* child. Once an alter is established by dissociation, it becomes easier to rely on that defense again and make more alters. These can be modeled on anyone and anything—perhaps a character from television or a book, someone strong who can serve as a protector or playmate. Alters can be based on the perpetrator too. In this way, dissociation sequesters the frightening abuse memories from the main stream of consciousness. This allows the child to grow up with an illusion of normalcy and safety. However, the fear has not left. It remains alive in the background. The traumatic memories and the alters that have custody over them could surface at any time, leading to terror and embarrassment.

How does this understanding of DID help us to understand the separation? According to the Course, our minds are split. On the one hand, we remain as God created us, as the Christ, our one true Self. On the other, we identify with the ego and the body. The first is real, the other is not, but we are invested in both. In our unwillingness to relinquish the ego, we try to maintain both as real through dissociation. But this is an unstable state. Dissociation lets us live in the ego's delusion, unaware of our true Identity. "*The ego is nothing more than a part of your belief about yourself. Your other life has continued without interruption, and has been and always will be totally unaffected by your attempts to dissociate it.*"[7]

The end result is billions of humans who believe that the ego is their true self. It is confined to a body, as are others. These bodies are separate and potentially threatening or alluring. Each could be thought of as an alter within the fractured, dissociated mind of God's one Son.

The good news is that the Son is unaffected by the ego's illusions. Therefore, to remember our true Identity requires only that we undo the dissociation. As noted before, we must remove "*the blocks to the awareness of love's presence.*"[8] We do this by handing off our ego-based judgments to the Holy Spirit, accepting His interpretation of events instead of our own and thereby bringing them more in line with truth. This is the process the Course calls "forgiveness." By recognizing the sameness in all of our brother and sister "alters" we forgo dissociation and begin to integrate the seemingly separate parts of the Sonship. This is our role in the Atonement. To the extent we commit to it and practice forgiveness, fear will give way to peace.

When treating DID, the psychotherapist must be present for and care about *all* the alters, even the ones who threaten or refuse to participate in treatment. The therapist doesn't play favorites or disparage any of them—although she may question their behavior. The relationships she builds with each alter become the basis for dissolving the boundaries of dissociation and reintegrating the alters into one stable individual. In the same way, the Holy Spirit guides each of us to recognize the ways in which our minds reinforce separation so that we can make a different choice and let Him lead us to awakening to oneness.

Projection

Dissociation as a defense doesn't address the source of the problem. It does nothing to undo the separation. Rather, it reinforces it. This leaves us with another problem. We feel guilty for abandoning God. We assume (incorrectly) that God must be angry with us and that He will seek vengeance on us. These feelings are intolerable. We deal with them by projecting them outside the "self" we've invested in and reacting to them as if others were intent on harming us.

If only the loving thoughts of God's Son are the world's reality, the real world must be in his mind. His insane thoughts, too, must be in his mind, but an internal conflict of this magnitude he cannot tolerate. A split mind is endangered, and the recognition that it encompasses completely opposed thoughts within itself is intolerable. Therefore the mind projects the split, not the reality. Everything you perceive as the outside world is merely your attempt to maintain your ego identification, for everyone believes that identification is salvation. Yet consider what has happened, for thoughts do have consequences to the thinker. You have become at odds with the world as you perceive it, because you think it is antagonistic to you. This is a necessary consequence of what you have done. You have projected outward what is antagonistic to what is inward, and therefore you would have to perceive it this way. That is why you must realize that your hatred is in your mind and not outside it before you can get rid of it; and why you must get rid of it before you can perceive the world as it really is.[9]

The moment we invested in the separation, the mind of the Son was split. His reality remained unchanged, because it was created by God. It is eternal. But another part of the mind now perceives itself as separate. It projects the separation and the guilt it engenders onto others and reacts to *them* as if they were now out to seek vengeance and do harm. Given this, how could the mind *not* be fearful, ever vigilant against anticipated attack? The world becomes a frightening place, where attack and eventually death are inevitable.

5

The World

This world is the opposite of Heaven, being made to be its opposite, and everything here takes a direction exactly opposite of what is true.[1]

There is no world apart from what you wish, and herein lies your ultimate release. Change but your mind on what you want to see, and all the world must change accordingly.[2]

The great English poet William Wordsworth composed a famous sonnet titled "The World Is Too Much with Us." He made the point that we are too captivated, too wrapped up in worldly goals and endeavors, at the expense of our connection to nature and the spiritual.

If that was true in his time, how much more so today! Between the demands of work and home and the flood of emails, texts, and social media posts, it has become impossible to keep up and "get it all done." Still, we try. I sometimes spend hours online, neglecting my deeper need to remember that I am spirit and my goal is peace.

We take it as a given that the outside world is real and important. It is the playing field upon which we transact our lives. We believe it has the power to hurt us unless we plan very carefully, and even then, unanticipated disaster can strike at any moment. Workbook lesson 31 states, "*I am not the victim of the world I see.*" But if you've lost a job, run short of money, gotten into an accident, or suffered the death of someone you love, it's tough not to feel like a victim. For too many, the world seems unfair. Why should some do so well while others struggle? Yet, peel away the outer appearance of success in anyone—CEOs, presidents, athletes, influencers, Hollywood stars—and you will find suffering and regret in some aspects of their lives. They may be wealthy, but estranged from their children; successful, but depressed; popular, but deeply lonely.

The world offers pleasures and pain, triumphs and failures, order and chaos, beauty and horror. We pursue the positive and shun the negative. But no matter how successful, famous, healthy, or wealthy you happen to be, at the end death will claim you. Chase after the world's offerings and happiness will be elusive. Impermanent. Remember, the ego's motto is: "*Seek and do* not *find.*"[3] The world encourages the seeking, but not the finding.

And so he seeks . . . in a thousand ways and in a thousand places, each time believing it is there, and each time dis-

appointed in the end. "Seek but do not find" remains this world's stern decree, and no one who pursues the world's goals can do otherwise.[4]

What Is the World?

"Where did everything come from?"

"What's my purpose here?"

"What does God want from me?"

Almost everyone has asked these questions at one time or another. If you turn to Judeo-Christian religion and the Bible for answers, you will be instructed that the world was created by God in six days and humankind was appointed steward over God's marvelous creation. However, this understanding runs into serious problems when we consider the abundance of suffering and pain in the world, not to mention the fact that so many species survive by killing and eating other species. We rightly ask, how could a loving God have created such a world?

A Course in Miracles agrees that God could not have created any such world, and indeed God did not.

The world you perceive is a world of separation.[5]

The world you see is an illusion of a world. God did not create it, for what He creates must be eternal as Himself. Yet there is nothing in the world you see that will endure forever. Some things will last in time a little while longer than others. But the time will come when all things visible will have an end.[6]

What seems eternal all will have an end. The stars will disap-
pear, and night and day will be no more. All things that come
and go, the tides, the seasons and the lives of men; all things
that change with time and bloom and fade will not return.
Where time has set an end is not where the eternal is.[7]

God creates by extending His oneness. Therefore, His creations must be like Himself. God is eternal, loving, and whole. The world is ephemeral, capricious, and fragmented—totally unlike God. It cannot be God's creation. It is a fabrication of the separated mind of God's Son.

To treasure the world and its deceptive offerings, then, is to feed the separation. If you value even one of its goals, awakening becomes impossible, because you have embraced separation. This is one of the more difficult teachings of the Course, especially for newer students.

One of the questions we receive most often at the Foundation for Inner Peace goes something like this: "There is so much beauty in the world—sunsets, rainbows, puppies, and kittens—how could it not be real? How can I not enjoy it? How could it not be God's creation?"

I usually answer this with a question of my own: "Where does the beauty come from?" Is it intrinsic to the world? That is, does the beauty exist outside of and independent of your perception? Or does it arise from your mind? Would it still look beautiful to you if you'd just lost a loved one? Or if you were in great pain? If not, then your mind is clearly the determining factor in how you see the world.

It's also worth noting that the world's beauty is generally appreciated from a distance. Standing on a hilltop looking out over fields and forests, or atop a high sand dune fronting the ocean, is indeed inspiring, but up close, it's different. That verdant forest is choked with death and decay. Bugs and fungi thrive. Our perception is selective, focusing on the beautiful while overlooking what we'd find repellent.

Workbook lessons 29 and 30 give us a helpful way of understanding this. Lesson 29 states, "*God is in everything I see.*" This would seem to indicate that God or His essence is infused throughout the world, that it is beautiful in its own right, and so must be God's creation. Of course, if rainbows and waterfalls are part of God's creation, then so too are tornados, tsunamis, slums, concentration camps, and toxic waste dumps. These are less congruent with our notions of God as an all-loving Being, and we try to rationalize them away.

Workbook lesson 30 adds a qualifier that helps make sense of this conundrum: "*God is in everything I see because God is in my mind.*" The beauty we perceive "out there" in the world as well as the horrors have no existence of their own. They are a product of the mind. God did not create the world, but He did create our mind—not the ego-mind, but mind as spirit. (French uses the same word, *esprit*, for both *mind* and *spirit*.) Therefore, according to the Course, anything we perceive in the world is the result of our own mind and its beliefs. This is reminiscent of Shakespeare's line "There is nothing either good or bad but that thinking makes it so."[8] If I am tired and hungry and just want to get home at the end of a long day, hitting a traffic jam feels infuriating. If you're with someone you enjoy talking to, you hardly notice the traffic. It's a matter of context, a matter of how we think about it.

Theodicy Refuted

Theologians have wrestled with the problem of evil in the world for centuries, tying themselves in knots of twisted logic in the attempt to exculpate God from any responsibility for it. They have even given the problem a name: *theodicy*, the vindication of divine goodness in view of the presence of evil. None of the theological rationales are convincing. So the question remains, how can evil exist if God, Who is love, created the world?

A Course in Miracles has a simple yet powerful explanation for the problem posed by theodicy: God did *not* create the world. It is the private delusion of His Son. God knows nothing about the world, except that His communication with His Son has been impeded. God does not determine events; he does not reward or punish. All the evil and all the good we behold in the world comes from us, from our mind. It is our responsibility.

The world you made is therefore totally chaotic, governed by arbitrary and senseless "laws," and without meaning of any kind. For it is made out of what you do not want, projected from your mind because you are afraid of it. Yet this world is only in the mind of its maker, along with his real salvation. Do not believe it is outside of yourself, for only by recognizing where it is will you gain control over it. For you do have control over your mind, since the mind is the mechanism of decision.[9]

Whatever you accept into your mind has reality for you. It is your acceptance of it that makes it real. If you enthrone the ego in your mind, your allowing it to enter makes it your reality.[10]

This is one of the Course's central lessons: we are responsible for what we experience. To change the world, it is not necessary to take action (unless we're so guided). Rather, we must change our mind about the world and the people we encounter.

The world you see is what you gave it, nothing more than that. But though it is no more than that, it is not less. Therefore, to you it is important. It is the witness to your state of mind, the outside picture of an inward condition. As a man thinketh, so does he perceive. Therefore, seek not to change the world, but choose to change your mind about the world. Perception is a result and not a cause.[11]

The mind is where change must occur. However, we are so locked into our beliefs, so wedded to the meaning we give our perceptions—the things we see and hear—that it is not possible to change our mind on our own. We need help. The Holy Spirit is that help. He abides in the mind, where the change must occur. The Course refers to Him as our remaining communication link to God. His task is to take our misinformed perceptions and translate them into truth, or at least move them in that direction. In doing so, our grievances and upsets disappear. Either they reveal themselves as something other than what we'd initially thought, or they simply vanish. But the Holy Spirit cannot accomplish this without our willingness. Therefore, our task is first to identify our unloving thoughts and perceptions as they arise and then, rather than enshrining them as true and making plans based on our faulty judgments, to hand them off to the Holy Spirit for his help. We want His interpretation, not ours. He sees only love and the loving. All else is illusion; it does not exist, because God did not create it. As we've noted, this is the process the Course calls "forgiveness."

Here's an example of how forgiveness can work. It may seem small and insignificant, but as the Course reminds us, there is no order of difficulty when it comes to miracles. Hierarchical structures and preferences belong to the world of form. They have no place in the oneness of God. Indeed, there are no parts within oneness to compare and rank order. I actually like "small" examples because we can all embrace them as possible for us. "Big" miracles and powerful forgiveness stories can inspire us, but they may leave us feeling inferior and dispirited: "How could something like that ever happen to me?" The more incredible the story, the less capable we feel of ever experiencing something similar. With that in mind, here's my example.

Just the other day, I saw a news article about a young man who wrote social media posts and created YouTube videos in support of a former president and his party, neither of whom I'm fond of. I felt a surge of rage well up in me. I did not wish this young man well. Instantly I recognized my attack thoughts and their effect on me. I "gave" them to the Holy Spirit for correction. I then proceeded to read the article. It turned out that this young man had seen the error of his ways. Not only had he stopped creating online content that risked provoking violence, but he was now devoted to exposing the inflammatory lies and malign intent behind such posts. Mentally, I apologized to him and thanked him.

I decided to change my mind and release my judgments about this man, whom I didn't even know—and he changed. The world changed.

No doubt many will scoff at this as nonsense. The world didn't change; it was just a coincidence. Yet I've experienced enough of these "coincidences" to become convinced that they are more than happenstance. In fact, the more the political process grinds to a frustrating, polarized standstill, I have come to see forgiveness and the Holy Spirit as the only meaningful way to effect real change.

But we must never forget that the beneficiary of our forgiveness is first ourselves, and secondly everyone else. When I choose to partner with the Holy Spirit in practicing forgiveness, I am kinder, more peaceful, more loving. My attitude affects everyone around me. According to the Course, it also potentially impacts people I've never even met, because minds are joined. (In truth, all minds are one.)

Perception and the World

The moment we attempt to discuss the nature of the world, we encounter a problem. Inherent in any discussion is our belief that the world is objectively real: a thing separate and apart from us. It is "out there," existing independently of the mind that perceives it. This belief supports and is supported by the separation, and it is very hard to overcome. We've spent years, decades even, learning how to see, hear, smell, taste, and touch and interpreting the messages these senses bring to us. Now *A Course in Miracles* tells us that we have to let go of our belief in the world, because it is false and will stand in the way of truth and real knowledge. It is perception that locks in our certainty about the world; it is therefore perception that must change.

> *Perception selects, and makes the world you see. It literally picks it out as the mind directs. . . . Perception is a choice and not a fact.*[12]

If we accept the truth of this statement, it is profoundly and powerfully liberating. As we noted earlier, we are not passive victims of life's vicissitudes. We are active participants. We have a choice in how we see the world and those who inhabit it. Are they rivals, threats, intent on taking all we have and leaving us for dead? Or are they brothers, fellow aspects of the greater Self that is our true reality, and as such identical to us? We are spirit; so are they. We are the Son of God; so are they. To God, we are one and the same. Here in the ego's world we appear to be different: in our appearance and personality, our needs, our past history, and our aspirations and goals. But those are elements of the dream of separation. They have no ultimate reality, because God did not create them.

The insight that perception makes the world returns power to us. We are the agents of our own imprisonment. Logically, then, we are also the agents of our own awakening. It only requires a change of mind. When we accept the fact that we remain as God created us—that the separation changed nothing—then all our perceived "sins" are "forgiven," because we acknowledge that they never occurred in the first place. Our delusional dream and the world it brought about have had no effect on God's reality or that of His Son. We remain innocent and holy.

This realization does not help us until we learn to accept it as truth. Not an easy task. However, when we experience miracles that defy the laws of cause and effect, laws by which the world is governed, it becomes increasingly difficult to sustain a belief in the world's objective reality.

The Course tells us that one goal of its curriculum is to undo perception and replace it with a different way of seeing, which it calls "Christ's vision." If perception keeps us locked into the world of separation, then its undoing opens the door to God and truth.

In *From Never-Mind to Ever-Mind*, I offered a number of exercises to help unravel our dependency on what we perceive and demonstrate just how unreliable it really is. We may not be able to "unsee" what the body's eyes show us, but we can choose to overlook those aspects that promote judgment and separation. Once we recognize that the differences we perceive are merely part of the dream, we can divest from them. If we recognize that we don't know the meaning of anything here in the world, we leave the door open for the Holy Spirit's interpretation. He sees only love and, if it's not love, then it's a cry for help and healing, whatever form it takes. Accept His interpretation as your own, and you will no longer be a slave to your judgments and perceptions. You will see with Christ's vision and become ripe for miracles.

Only the Past

Why is our perception of the world so prone to inaccuracy? Workbook lesson 7 holds the answer: we *"see only the past."* But the past is over; it is not now. Therefore, its usefulness in guiding our judgments is severely limited.

The notion that we see only the past may seem counterintuitive. Look around and what you see appears to be present *now*. But it's only given meaning by the past. (This was the topic of chapter 2 in *From Never-Mind to Ever-Mind*.) We see a spoon, a car, a tree, and recognize them by our past experience of spoons, cars, and trees. Each seems to have its proper place. If a spoon, car, or tree were to turn up in a bank, for example, it would be confusing, startling even.

In most instances, our perceptions are benign: they do not trigger us into either fear or desire. We have no need to avoid them or crave and pursue them. But this is not true for our perception of other people, whom we judge in all sorts of ways: by how they look and speak, whom they know, where they went to school, what kind of car they drive, what work they perform, and what we think they can do for us. Our judgments turn into attacks all too easily. Or we confer upon the "other" a sense of specialness. Either way, the belief that they are separate and different from us is strengthened. The moment their behavior deviates from what we have expected from them, a grievance is born. Rely on your own flawed judgment, and grievances are inevitable. By the time we reach adulthood, they are so dense and ingrained that we cannot see them for what they are and release them. We have become slaves to our own system of beliefs, rooted in the past.

I have discussed the Buddhist concept of beginner's mind in my other books. The term refers to the ability to suspend judgment and greet each situation and person as if for the first time. If we could meet each person with no preconceptions, desiring to see only the truth in them, only their holiness, what might that be like?

> Be innocent of judgment, unaware of any thoughts of evil or of good that ever crossed your mind of anyone. Now do you know him not. But you are free to learn of him, and learn of him anew. Now is he born again to you, and you are born again to him, without the past that sentenced him to die, and you with him. Now is he free to live as you are free, because an ancient learning passed away, and left a place for truth to be reborn.[13]

The Course reminds us repeatedly that by relinquishing our judgments in the understanding that they are always faulty, we benefit not only others, but ourselves. Ultimately, this leads to a recognition of our fundamental similarity. Light and holiness are present in everyone, no matter their personality or their past misdeeds. This promotes love and compassion instead of competition, attack, sacrifice, and bargaining.

> *When you meet anyone, remember it is a holy encounter. As you see him you will see yourself. As you treat him you will treat yourself. As you think of him you will think of yourself. Never forget this, for in him you will find yourself or lose yourself. Whenever two Sons of God meet, they are given another chance at salvation. Do not leave anyone without giving salvation to him and receiving it yourself.*[14]

Without the past, you have no basis for judgment. No thing is reminiscent of any other thing; nobody reminds you of someone else who hurt you, or whom you loved and lost. As the Course quote above states, you now see your brother with the vision of the Holy Spirit, which frees both him and you from illusion. Recognizing the light of holiness in him, you discover that same light in yourself.

* * *

Undoing the past is the goal of the Atonement. It teaches that our reality lies only in the present moment. By embracing the present and relinquishing the past, we also release the future. Otherwise, the die of the future has been cast in the past, and we are more or less guaranteed to repeat it. There is no way out of this time loop other than the present moment. "*The present* is *forgiveness.*"[15] This is so because without the past grievances have no basis. They are no more. That is what the Atonement promises.

> Atonement teaches you how to escape forever from every-thing that you have taught yourself in the past, by showing you only what you are now.[16]

> Atonement might be equated with total escape from the past and total lack of interest in the future. Heaven is here. There is nowhere else. Heaven is now. There is no other time.[17]

The Holy Spirit and Jesus are tasked with bringing the Atone-ment to completion. Without their help, the past would remain too real, too fixed and compelling in our minds, and forgiveness nearly impossible. But Jesus and the Holy Spirit cannot help without our willingness. We have an essential part to play. Our part is to take note of every unforgiving thought we have and give them all to the Holy Spirit for His interpretation. The sooner we identify them for what they are, the sooner we can be free of their dark influence. That might take mere seconds or stretch to encompass decades, but the time it takes is less important than the intention and effort. Once aware of a grievance, why continue to carry it around with you? It's not doing anything positive, and it is destructive to your peace of mind.

Like any new skill, this process of awareness and release requires practice and commitment. You will forget. Often. You will continue to judge. Those grievances will sneak past your radar, and you will have attack thoughts. And over time you will learn. Patience and perseverance yield dividends. As the Course tells us, *"This is a course in mind training."*[18] We must train our minds to reverse the training of the ego that we were raised with. When we do, the world will look very different. We will see and move about in what the Course calls "the real world": the staging ground for the final return to God.

6

The Real World

The real world is the state of mind in which the only purpose of the world is seen to be forgiveness.[1]

You will first dream of peace, and then awaken to it.[2]

When we allow the Holy Spirit to judge for us, our perceptions shift. We no longer see the world as a collection of separate objects, bodies, and events—or if we do, we no longer credit them as real. We have learned to "see" (though not with the body's eyes) the light of holiness in each being. Recognizing it in them, we can also recognize it in our selves. This naturally leads to a sense of joining and union, because we see that the light in them is the same as the light in us. It is more real and more compelling than anything we'll ever perceive in the ego's world.

The Course refers to the "real world" frequently, but the concept has proven confusing to many students. If there is a real world behind the world of appearances, then wouldn't God have had to create it? Is it just the ego's world that we must look past? Or is the entire world as perceived by our five senses an illusion to be passed by, a dream from which we must awaken, if we're ever to find lasting happiness? The distinction is important.

Unfortunately, a few lines scattered throughout the Course seem to imply that God does in fact have some role in the real world. However, taken in the context of the Course's entire teaching, this cannot be the case.

The world as you perceive it cannot have been created by the Father, for the world is not as you see it. God created only the eternal, and everything you see is perishable. Therefore, there must be another world that you do not see.[3]

On the first reading, this quote seems to say that there is a world beyond perception, one that's eternal and known and loved by God. However, a central tenet of the Course is that God knows nothing of the separation. The separation gave birth to the world; therefore God does not and cannot play any role in its formation. God is the totality of everything real, and God is love and only love. There is no room in God for anything but love. How then could God carve out wholeness to create a "real world"?

God knows only Himself and His creations, that is, His Son (as well as the Son's creations). That is all there is. However, God did give us a way out of the ego's world:

the Atonement. The Holy Spirit and Jesus are in charge of this escape route—the Holy Spirit, because He remains eternally in Heaven as part of the mind of the Sonship, and Jesus because he awoke fully to his true Self, the Christ, which is the Self we all share despite the separation.

> *It is not God you have imprisoned in your plan to lose your Self. He does not know about a plan so alien to His Will. There was a need He did not understand, to which He gave an Answer. That is all. And you who have this Answer given you have need no more of anything but this.*[4]

The Atonement undoes the world perception shows us. Once this is accomplished, there are no more blocks to awakening, and we naturally welcome God to rejoin with us. However, if this were to take place instantly, it would be terrifying for all but a rare few. We remain far too invested in our ego identity, our body, and our life story to happily let them go. We need to move in steps. And we need to move toward an experience that offers more than anything the world can offer. The Course can make all sorts of promises, but these are merely words and open to doubt. When you have an experience of light, love, or mystical oneness, you will know beyond any doubt that it is more real than anything the world can offer. It becomes the only thing you want. Achieving this experience is the goal of the Course's training. *"A universal theology is impossible, but a universal experience is not only possible but necessary. It is this experience toward which the course is directed."*[5]

With this in mind, the best way to understand the real world is as a way station along the road to enlightenment. As long as we remain attached to our bodies and our ego identities, the idea of giving these up will seem fearful. We equate this seeming loss of self with death, so it is a thing to be feared and avoided. The Holy Spirit cannot teach through fear. Fear is antithetical to love. Therefore, instead of one big leap into oneness, the Atonement proceeds in smaller steps, which are perfectly matched to our readiness by the Holy Spirit. Fear need never enter. Our self-concept is slowly and gradually eroded in favor of a more truthful one, which brings joy.

> *Now must the Holy Spirit find a way to help you see this concept of the self must be undone, if any peace of mind is to be given you. Nor can it be unlearned except by lessons aimed to teach that you are something else. For otherwise, you would be asked to make exchange of what you now believe for total loss of self, and greater terror would arise in you.*
>
> *Thus are the Holy Spirit's lesson plans arranged in easy steps, that though there be some lack of ease at times and some distress, there is no shattering of what was learned, but just a re-translation of what seems to be the evidence on its behalf.*[6]

If perception is the great perpetuator of separation, then its undoing is the necessary prerequisite for awakening. False perception gives way to true perception. To the extent that all perception is false, this is an oxymoron. But it is what we need to return home. This process unfolds at a pace uniquely suited to our beliefs and circumstances, such that fear is pacified and joy welcomed with increasingly less resistance.

The real world is simply that state of mind in which true perception reigns. Forgiveness is complete. It rests upon all people and all perceptions, perceiving no differences and making no judgments based on the past. Every circumstance is judged not by us, but by the Holy Spirit, and seen with His forgiving vision. The body's eyes may continue to see separation, but the mind does not.

"The world you see must be denied, for sight of it is costing you a different kind of vision. You cannot see both worlds, *for each of them involves a different kind of seeing, and depends on what you cherish. The sight of one is possible because you have denied the other."*[7]

This teaching is repeated throughout the Course, for example, in Workbook lessons 128 through 130. *"The world I see holds nothing that I want"*; *"Beyond this world there is a world I want"*; and *"It is impossible to see two worlds."* Lessons 170 and 171 state, *"I will not use the body's eyes today"* and *"Christ's is the vision I will use."* If we gaze upon a world of differences, of distinct people, objects, and events, we cannot forgive—not as the Course defines forgiveness. The best we can do is to acknowledge sin and grievance as real and then pretend to overlook them from a stance of righteous superiority. But that is not true forgiveness. It will not lead to a vision of the real world. For that, we need Christ's vision.

Christ's Vision

The body's eyes are incapable of seeing anything real, that is, anything created by God. They are organs of perception. As such, they bring to us what we have projected outward to escape our guilt about the separation.

Christ's vision is different. It does not see bodies or differences. It looks past the illusions of separation that perception brings us through the five senses.

> *Christ's vision has one law. It does not look upon a body, and mistake it for the Son whom God created. It beholds a light beyond the body; an idea beyond what can be touched; a purity undimmed by errors, pitiful mistakes, and fearful thoughts of guilt from dreams of sin. It sees no separation. And it looks on everyone, on every circumstance, all happenings and all events, without the slightest fading of the light it sees.*[8]

> *Christ's vision is a miracle. It comes from far beyond itself, for it reflects eternal love and the rebirth of love which never dies, but has been kept obscure. Christ's vision pictures Heaven, for it sees a world so like to Heaven that what God created perfect can be mirrored there.*[9]

When we view the world through Christ's vision, everything in it appears radiant and beautiful, because it reflects the radiance and beauty of our own mind as God created it. We see the world and all in it as the Holy Spirit sees it, registering only what is loving. In His sight, *there is nothing else to* be seen, because there *is* nothing else. If it's not love, if God did not create it, then it does not exist. The Holy Spirit sees only what exists. He does not bolster the world we made by joining in our false perceptions. Rather, He brings our perceptions into alignment with love. He brings illusion to truth. This leads to Christ's vision and the real world.

> *Do not seek vision through your eyes, for you made your way of seeing that you might see in darkness, and in this you are deceived. Beyond this darkness, and yet still within you, is the vision of Christ, Who looks on all in light. Your "vision" comes from fear, as His from love. And He sees for you, as your witness to the real world.*[10]

This is our sole purpose here in the world. "*Your purpose is to see the world through your own holiness. Thus are you and the world blessed together.*"[11] We substitute Christ's healing vision, imparted through the Holy Spirit, for our own flawed sight.

How is Christ's vision achieved? The answer is simple: through forgiveness. Through the release of the past and all it represents. It is impossible to be at peace, much less to teach peace by our example, if we buy into a world of conflict and attack. What we behold in our brothers and sisters will necessarily be true for ourselves as well. If they are threatening, then so are we. If they have suspicious ulterior motives, then so do we. If we do not trust them, it's a safe bet that they don't trust us either.

Understood in this way, forgiveness is a win-win proposition. We are not asked to sacrifice our righteous indignation or to trash our cherished self-concept. We are asked to let go of these views because they are wrong. They show us our brothers as bodies, obscuring the light of holiness that is their true being. When we forgive, that light shines forth as their only reality. They are released from our judgments—and so are we! *"Whom you forgive is given power to forgive you your illusions. By your gift of freedom is it given unto you."*[12]

Through forgiveness we attain Christ's vision. And in Christ's vision, nothing can be seen that's undeserving of forgiveness. You and your brother are spirit, not bodies. You are the same, created as one by the same loving Creator. It is impossible to hold a grudge when you see your brother this way, bathed in the light of truth.

Forgiveness is the only thing that stands for truth in the illusions of the world. It sees their nothingness. . . . It looks on lies, but it is not deceived.[13]

And as our focus goes beyond mistakes, we will behold a wholly sinless world. When seeing this is all we want to see, when this is all we seek for in the name of true perception, are the eyes of Christ inevitably ours. And the Love He feels for us becomes our own as well. This will become the only thing we see reflected in the world and in ourselves.[14]

In Christ's sight, the world and God's creation meet, and as they come together all perception disappears.[15]

How Will the World End?

For most people, the thought of perception disappearing remains frightening. Ask anyone who's taken a large dose of LSD what it's like when the familiar world that you believed to be stable and real begins to melt and fade away. It's disconcerting, to say the least! For this reason, Western religion has cast the end of the world in a terrifying light. God descends, angry and vengeful, to judge the world and everyone in it. Should He find any of them unworthy, they are barred from Heaven and cast into the eternal blast furnace of hell.

The Course offers a very different view of the end of the world, one far more compatible with a God of Love.

The final judgment on the world contains no condemnation. For it sees the world as totally forgiven, without sin and wholly purposeless. Without a cause, and now without a function in Christ's sight, it merely slips away to nothingness. There it was born, and there it ends as well. And all the figures in the dream in which the world began go with it. Bodies now are useless, and will therefore fade away, because the Son of God is limitless.

You who believed that God's Last Judgment would condemn the world to hell along with you, accept this holy truth: God's Judgment is the gift of the Correction He bestowed on all your errors, freeing you from them, and all effects they ever seemed to have. To fear God's saving grace is but to fear complete release from suffering, return to peace, security and happiness, and union with your own Identity.

God's Final Judgment is as merciful as every step in His appointed plan to bless His Son, and call him to return to the eternal peace He shares with him. . . .

This is God's Final Judgment: "You are still My holy Son, forever innocent, forever loving and forever loved, as limitless as your Creator, and completely changeless and forever pure. Therefore awaken and return to Me. I am your Father and you are My Son."[16]

If we could accept this vision of the end of the world instead of the fearful apocalyptic vision promulgated by most Christian traditions, we would rush to embrace it. The main obstacle in our way is our false and limited self-concept and the world it believes it inhabits. As these become less compelling and the alternative ever more convincing based on our experience, our resistance diminishes. The sight of the real world may not be as awe-inspiring as the experience of revelation, but it is so lovely and captivating that it becomes our benchmark for assessing the validity of all we perceive. The more we look on the real world, the harder it becomes to sustain belief in the ego's world. Finally we realize it is no sacrifice to give up what was never real (and can never be).

Decide but to accept your rightful place as co-creator of the universe, and all you think you made will disappear. What rises to awareness then will be all that there ever was, eternally as it is now.[17]

The world will end in joy, because it is a place of sorrow. When joy has come, the purpose of the world has gone. The world will end in peace, because it is a place of war. When peace has come, what is the purpose of the world? The world will end in laughter, because it is a place of tears. Where there is laughter, who can longer weep? And only complete forgiveness brings all this to bless the world. In blessing it departs, for it will not end as it began.[18]

The end of the world is not its destruction, but its translation into Heaven. The reinterpretation of the world is the transfer of all perception to knowledge.[19]

God's Final Step

The real world represents a short-term, intermediate goal; it is not the finish line for the Course's curriculum, although it is a necessary prerequisite. If we continue to value the things of the ego's world, if we see the world of perception as the only available option for finding happiness, then we will never find it. The very nature of the separation makes this impossible. As the introduction to the Text makes clear right at the outset, love is our natural inheritance. It is eternal and ever present. We don't have to *do* anything to experience it. No action is capable of bringing us Heaven, because actions involve bodies and occur in the outer world. If we rely on action to free us, we are paradoxically reinforcing the reality of the dream world we're trying to awaken from. "*Enlightenment is but a recognition, not a change at all.*"[20]

To awaken to the real world, and from there to reality as God created it, we must disavow our ordinary perception and the false picture of the world it portrays. Once this has been accomplished, what we will behold (through Christ's vision) is the real world.

The Course tells us that the vision of the real world does not last long. With all obstacles to the awareness of Love's presence removed, nothing stands in the way of our remembering God and returning to Him. With no investment in the world of time and bodies, our sole desire is for God. And God answers by welcoming us back to wholeness.

> *The perception of the real world will be so short that you will barely have time to thank God for it. For God will take the last step swiftly, when you have reached the real world and have been made ready for Him.*[21]

Of course, time does not exist in the real world, so the idea that anything will last, however briefly, is itself part of the illusion. It is unthinkable to the holy Son of God, Who abides in a perfect, eternal present. Were we to grow attached to the vision of the real world and try to keep it, it would become an obstacle to the remembrance of God. It would cease to *be* the real world anymore!

Once no further obstacles remain to block awakening, God instantly sweeps us up into His metaphoric arms and takes what the Course calls the "final step," in which perception gives way to knowledge and the oneness of Heaven is restored.

> *The swiftness with which your new and only real perception will be translated into knowledge will leave you but an*

instant to realize that this alone is true. And then everything
you made will be forgotten; the good and the bad, the false
and the true. For as Heaven and earth become one, even the
real world will vanish from your sight.[22]

Does this seem frightening to you? If so, it is only because you are still attached to your self-concept and the ego that feeds it. That's OK. So am I. So is everyone on earth (with the possible exception of a very few). If you're still here in a body, you very likely have not yet awakened. There are still lessons to be learned, obstacles to love's presence that still must be recognized and uprooted.

Remember, though, the Holy Spirit is in charge of the pace of learning, not you, not your partner, not the leader of your Course in Miracles group. This should be deeply reassuring. The Holy Spirit knows your readiness for each step in learning to accept the Atonement. His lessons are perfectly calibrated to your stage of understanding. He cannot teach through fear. If you feel fear, it can only come from the ego. View it as another opportunity to recognize its source and release it. Nothing more than that is needed. You are perfectly protected and perfectly safe—far more so than if you lived your life out as a body, in ignorance of the Course and the Holy Spirit.

The real world is the short-term goal. We get there through our consistent and determined practice of forgiveness. But God is the ultimate goal. This is why the real world is a layover and will not last long. We have paved the way for God to enter. Why ever would He hesitate?

And thus is God left free to take the final step Himself. . . . Forgiveness vanishes and symbols fade, and nothing that the eyes have ever seen or ears have heard remains to be perceived. A power wholly limitless has come, not to destroy, but to receive its own. There is no choice of function anywhere. . . . Give welcome to the power beyond forgiveness, and beyond the world of symbols and of limitations. He would merely be, and so He merely is.[23]

7

Decision

The very last section of the Text of *A Course in Miracles* is titled "Choose Once Again." After more than six hundred pages covering topics like love, forgiveness, salvation, Christ's vision, Atonement, and relationships special and holy, the final emphasis is on decision.

Of course, that emphasis is present throughout the Course, and for a very good reason. We are wandering blindly, lost in ego dreams. We are so lost that we are unable to extricate ourselves without help. That help, Who is the Holy Spirit, can do nothing for us without our willingness. He needs our invitation to enter our lives and correct our perception and interpretation of the world. This in turn requires us to make a decision. We must choose to hear His Voice while ignoring the ego's.

Back at the beginning of time, the Son of God made a choice to separate from God. He chose specialness over love. That choice was an impossible one because the Son's very identity as God created Him is love. Therefore love and God cannot *not* be a part of us. The choice to separate had no real, lasting effects except in the mind of the Son Himself. However, it remains powerful to the extent that we continue to choose to believe we are separate beings. We must let go of all we made and tried to invest with reality in our dedication to separation and then actively choose to return to our true Self in God. In fact, this is the *only* thing required of us. *"The power of decision is your one remaining freedom as a prisoner of this world."*[1]

This means that the thousands of decisions we make regarding the world and our place in it are not truly decisions at all. Why? Because they have no effect on our reality. We merely shuffle off one illusion and grab hold of another in the hope that it will somehow be different and satisfy us in ways the last one failed to do. This is not choice, as all alternatives keep us stuck in illusion. Choosing a different prison cell will not free you from prison. The only *real* choice we're capable of making, the only one that counts, is between God and ego, spirit and body, truth and illusion.

> It is still up to you to choose to join with truth or with illusion. But remember that to choose one is to let the other go. Which one you choose you will endow with beauty and reality, because the choice depends on which you value more. The spark of beauty or the veil of ugliness, the real world or the world of guilt and fear, truth or illusion, freedom or slavery—it is all the same. For you can never choose except between God and the ego.[2]

The Holy Spirit, like the ego, is a decision. Together they constitute all the alternatives the mind can accept and obey. The Holy Spirit and the ego are the only choices open to you. God created one, and so you cannot eradicate it. You made the other, and so you can. Only what God creates is irreversible and unchangeable. What you made can always be changed because, when you do not think like God, you are not really thinking at all. Delusional ideas are not real thoughts, although you can believe in them. But you are wrong.[3]

We are confronted with hundreds of decisions even in the space of a single day. Most seem very minor, almost trivial, such as what clothes to wear in the morning or what to eat. Others are more significant, like where to go to school, which jobs to apply for, or whether to undergo surgery or not. However, recall the first miracle principle: *"There is no order of difficulty in miracles. One is not 'harder' or 'bigger' than another. They are all the same."*[4] Likewise, Workbook lesson 79 tells us that, although we perceive problems of all varieties in multiple areas of our lives, there is really only a single problem which lies at the root of all them, namely, the separation from God. Because we identify with a physical body that lives within a threatening world where it is doomed to die, we are ever on the alert, vigilant against danger, making plans to control the future. We eat healthily, we exercise, we take medications, we install alarms and buy guns, and we try to save money for unexpected emergencies. None of our plans will work, however, because the body was not created by God. It is an aspect of the world of illusion. As such, it must age and die.

Whatever seeming choices we make within the world of illusion, none will awaken us. You cannot dispel illusions by choosing a different illusion. In fact, each one subtly reinforces our belief in the world's false reality. The Course is very clear that holding on to even a single cherished illusion will keep you from awakening. They must all be recognized for what they are (and what they are not), and ultimately released to the Holy Spirit for reinterpretation. This is why it is a course in undoing. Your reality is unchangeable: safe, and perfectly preserved. It is your illusions that must be lifted because they block you from true sight or Christ's vision.

> *You need to be reminded that you think a thousand choices are confronting you, when there is really only one to make. And even this but seems to be a choice. Do not confuse yourself with all the doubts that myriad decisions would induce. You make but one. And when that one is made, you will perceive it was no choice at all. For truth is true, and nothing else is true. There is no opposite to choose instead. There is no contradiction to the truth.*[5]

> *Could it be some dreams are kept, and others wakened from? The choice is not between which dreams to keep, but only if you want to live in dreams or to awaken from them.*[6]

Decision is further complicated by our belief that we're capable of making good decisions for ourselves. We rely on our own personal judgment, but it is based on past experience. This has the unfortunate effect of keeping the past alive in our minds. We shape the future in alignment with the past, leaving little or no space for real change. We remain willfully blind to our brothers' true nature, preferring to see them as separate and in competition with us, or in certain special instances, collaborating. But any alliances are temporary, as collaboration can quickly give way to competition. As a result, we can never be fully comfortable or confident in any of our relationships. Behind every decision we make on our own, there lurks fear.

As noted previously, we need help to discriminate between truth and illusion. God created the Holy Spirit for precisely this purpose. He and He alone is in a position to see both truth and illusion. When we ask Him to help us choose, He will lead us away from false choices between illusions and toward the one truth. For this to be effective, we must accept first that we are incapable of making sound judgments, and second, that the Holy Spirit *is* capable. We therefore relinquish decision making to Him.

Say to the Holy Spirit only, "Decide for me," and it is done. For His decisions are reflections of what God knows about you, and in this light, error of any kind becomes impossible. Why would you struggle so frantically to anticipate all you cannot know, when all knowledge lies behind every decision the Holy Spirit makes for you? Learn of His wisdom and His Love, and teach His answer to everyone who struggles in the dark.[7]

Before you make any decisions for yourself, remember that you have decided against your function in Heaven, and then consider carefully whether you want to make decisions here. Your function here is only to decide against deciding what you want, in recognition that you do not know. How, then, can you decide what you should do? Leave all decisions to the One Who speaks for God, and for your function as He knows it.[8]

The Course is telling us that, despite what we've come to believe, there is really only one decision to be made, ever—about anything. We choose the spirit or the body, the ego or the Holy Spirit, reality or illusions. Again, the emphasis is on "unlearning." If we continue to think we know the best answers, or even an approximation of what's "right," we leave no opening for the Holy Spirit. Instead, we affirm the separation and our role in it. As a result, we will remain asleep and dreaming.

We rarely if ever recognize the one decision underlying the many that confront us. But as the Bible and the Course both remind us, "By their fruits ye shall know them, and they shall know themselves."[9] Decide with the ego, and the outcome will bring no happiness. Decide with the Holy Spirit, and happiness is the inevitable result, even though it may arrive in forms that you never could have imagined. Seen clearly, who among us would not choose happiness?

What does this mean in practical terms? On the big decisions it is wise to consult the Holy Spirit. In fact, it is essential! But is it necessary to ask Him about every little thing? You could, but is it helpful? Many decisions are rather trivial in that they have no significant consequences.

Rather than compulsively asking about every decision, far better to awaken in the morning and give your day to the Holy Spirit in advance. Then remember to affirm your reality as spirit all through the day. To the extent you can put this into practice, your decisions will seem to take care of themselves, easily, with little to no effort on your part.

Our task as Course students is therefore to decide *against* deciding in the understanding that (1) we're incapable of it and that (2) the decisions we think we face are illusory, rooted as they are in the ego and its world. When the ship is sinking, does it matter what color your lifeboat is painted? The only thing that matters is getting yourself a seat on board.

If your five-year-old child insisted she should drive the car, you'd gently but firmly tell her that's not possible. You would not allow her to put herself and others in danger just to satisfy a whim. You, the adult, can drive her wherever she needs to go with far greater safety and confidence. Our situation with respect to the Holy Spirit is similar. He knows how to decide in our best interests; we do not. Let's leave the driving to Him!

Decide for One, Decide for All

Your belief in your unique, individual self is a shabby construct, a fiction perpetrated by the ego and designed to keep your true identity in God unremembered. Any decision you make arising from this fiction will be very limited in its ability to help. More likely, it will hurt by keeping you asleep and dreaming.

The implications of this truth are staggering. They may even seem insane at first. It is only in their application, as you perceive their results, that their truth is established. All decisions you make alone, about any subject, will be unhelpful, because their fundamental premise is incorrect. You are not an individual. Your true Self, along with everyone else's, is the Son of God. Having forgotten this, you need the Holy Spirit, Who has not and will not forget, to choose for you.

> *It is not true that you can make decisions by yourself or for yourself alone. No thought of God's Son can be separate or isolated in its effects. Every decision is made for the whole Sonship, directed in and out, and influencing a constellation larger than anything you ever dreamed of.* [10]

This might seem to impose a huge obligation on us. As Workbook lesson 238 states, "*On my decision, all salvation rests.*" So are we responsible for *everyone*? Yes . . . and no. Any conviction we hold about the impossibility of salvation is merely another example of the ego and its countermeasures against salvation.

Yes, you are responsible for the entire Sonship, because that is your true Identity. But you have help in the Holy Spirit, Who was created by God for this purpose. Because it is God's will that you accept Atonement and awaken, it is done. You do not have the power to contravene what God wills. All that remains unanswered is how long this takes within the world of time, and that is ultimately irrelevant, because time is part of the illusion. From the perspective of eternity, it is already accomplished.

> *By teaching what to choose, the Holy Spirit will ultimately teach you that you need not choose at all. This will finally liberate your mind from choice, and direct it towards creation within the Kingdom.*
>
> *Choosing through the Holy Spirit will lead you to the Kingdom. You create by your true being, but what you are you must learn to remember.*[11]

In the oneness of Heaven there is no need for choice. There are no differences and no options. All is union and bliss. Until we reach this stage, however, choosing with the Holy Spirit is our only function here in the world. This is because it is the only path out of illusion and confusion.

*   *   *

A Course in Miracles is holographic. What is true for the part—the seemingly separate, individual self—must also be true for the whole. Why? Because *there are no parts* within the Sonship. It is one. Each "part" is simultaneously the whole. *"The recognition of the part as whole, and of the whole in every part is perfectly natural, for it is the way God thinks, and what is natural to Him is natural to you."*[12] This helps make sense of Workbook lesson 137, which states, *"When I am healed, I am not healed alone."* True healing as the Course teaches it can only mean the undoing of the separation and reinstatement of the awareness of our true

Self. When we accomplish this for our "individual" self, we are also helping to heal the entire Sonship of its delusion of separation.

Given the Course's understanding of the nature of self, this makes perfect sense. If each of us is both a part and the whole of the collective Christ mind, whatever healing we accomplish will affect both levels. We believe we are separate, so we must address this delusion first by accepting Atonement for ourselves. However, in reality we are not separate. Our "individual" healing is but a necessary part of the healing of the entire Sonship, which constitutes our true Self. We heal ourselves by seeing our brothers and sisters as they truly are, through Christ's vision. This allows them in turn to view us in the same light. Separation gives way to joining and ultimately to union as bodies fade and spirit is recognized as our reality. But this cannot occur unless and until we choose it. We must *decide* that this is what we want, with no other goals or ego-based distractions. Therefore, it does not matter which relationships we choose to heal. We are lost, ignorant. Far better to let the Holy Spirit transform *all* of your relationships according to His knowledge and your readiness.

You see the flesh or recognize the spirit. There is no compromise between the two. If one is real the other must be false, for what is real denies its opposite. There is no choice in vision but this one. What you decide in this determines all you see and think is real and hold as true. On this one choice does all your world depend, for here have you established what you are, as flesh or spirit in your own belief. If you choose flesh, you never will escape the body as your own reality, for you have chosen that you want it so. But choose the spirit, and all Heaven bends to touch your eyes and bless your holy sight, that you may see the world of flesh no more except to heal and comfort and to bless.[13]

Notes

Direct quotations from *A Course in Miracles* are in italics; all emphasis is from the original. The notes use the standard reference numbering of *A Course in Miracles* as published by the Foundation for Inner Peace. This enables students to refer to a specific passage within the Course and its supplements. References are to the combined third edition (Tiburon, Calif.: Foundation for Inner Peace, 2007).

The key to the references is as follows:

T stands for the Text. **W** stands for the Workbook. **M** stands for the Manual for Teachers. **C** stands for Clarification of Terms (at the end of the Manual). **P** stands for *Psychotherapy: Purpose, Process, and Practice.* **S** stands for *The Song of Prayer.*

Here is an example:
"*You will first dream of peace, and then awaken to it*" (T-13.VII.9:1).

T = Text

13 = chapter 13

VII = section VII (of chapter 13)

9 = paragraph 9 (in section VII)

1 = line 1 (of paragraph 9)

Another example:

"*We say 'God is,' and then we cease to speak, for in that knowledge words are meaningless*" (W-pI.169.5:4).

W = Workbook

pI = part I (of the Workbook)

169 = lesson 169

5 = paragraph 5

4 = line 4 (of paragraph 5)

Page references to the same edition have been added for convenience.

Endnotes

Preface
1. Workbook lessons 94, 110, 112, 120, 162, 176, 201–220.
2. T-14.X.10:1, 10:7, p. 295.
3. W-pII.231.1:1–5, p. 408.
4. W-pII.318.1:5-7, p. 459.

Chapter 1. The Journey
1. T-8.VI.9:6–7, p. 150.
2. P-3. II. 8:8, p. 21.
3. T-2.I.3:6, p. 18.
4. T-13.VII.17:7, p. 257.
5. T-12.IV.5:1–2, p. 224.
6. T-12.IV.5:3, p. 224.
7. Robert Rosenthal, *From Plagues to Miracles: The Transformational Journey of Exodus, From the Slavery*

of Ego to the Promised Land of Spirit (Carlsbad, Calif.: Hay House, 2012), 24.

8. T-29.VII.1:1, p. 617.
9. T-11.VII.4:5, p. 210.
10. T-31.IV.10:4-8, p. 655.
11. T-26.V.9:8, p. 551.
12. W-155.11:1–4, p. 292.

Chapter 2. Freedom

1. T-10.IV.5:1–2, p. 188.
2. T-11.II.7:7, p. 198.
3. T-19.IVB.i.17:2, p. 416.
4. First Corinthians 13:12, King James Version.
5. T-22.VI.1:1–2, 8–2:1–2, p. 480.
6. T-14.IV.5:1–4, 6:1–2, p. 280.
7. T-24.VII.8:8–10, p. 516.
8. T-25.I.3:1–3, p. 519.
9. W.304.1:3–4, p. 451.
10. T-28.II.6:7, p. 591.
11. T-28.IV.5:4, p. 599.
12. T-17.III.1:1–3, p. 354.
13. T-14.XI.6:3–9, pp. 297–98.
14. T-20.III.9:1–2, p. 431.
15. T-22.II.4:4, p. 472.
16. W.313.1:1–2; 2:1–3, p. 457.
17. Philippians 4:7, King James Version.
18. T-13.VII.9:1–8, pp. 255–56.
19. T-17.II.1:1–5, 2:1–3, 5:1, pp. 352–53.
20. W-97.7:2, p. 173.
21. T-31.VI.3:1–4, p. 661.

22. T-29.IX.7.1–8, p. 623.
23. T-3.VI.11:1–5, p. 49.
24. T-30.II.2:1–3, p. 629.
25. T-13.VII.3:1–4:4, p. 254.

Chapter 3. The Body

1. T-15.IX.2:3, p. 322.
2. T-25.In.1:1–3, p. 518.
3. T-24.VII.9:1–10:1, p. 516.
4. W-229, p. 406.
5. T-18.VIII.1:1–2:6, p. 390.
6.   T-23.II.2:1, p. 489.
7. T-27.VIII.1:1–3:2, pp. 585–86.
8. T-6.V-A.5:3, p. 105.
9. T-19.IV.B, p. 412.
10. Personal communication from Bill Thetford to the author.
11. T-1.VII.1:2–4, p. 15.
12. T-17.VI.2:2, p. 366.
13. T-19.IV.B.i.12:1–4, p. 415.
14. T-1.I.1:1–4, p. 3.
15. Introduction.1:7, p. 1.
16. T-16.VI.8:1–2, p. 346.
17. T-26.VII.2:1, p. 554.
18. T-8.IX.3:2, p. 158.
19. W-136.8:1–9:1, p. 258.
20. M-5.II.2:1–3:2, p. 18.
21. W-158.7:1–5, p. 299.
22. T-8.VII.4:3, p. 151.
23. T-8.VII.3:1–2, p. 151.

24. T-2.V.5:1, pp. 25–26.
25. W-236, p. 410.
26. T-1.I.25:1, p. 4.
27. T-10.IV.7:5–6, p. 189.
28. T-14.III.9:4, p. 276.
29. T-8.VII.10:1, p. 153.
30. T-8.VIII.9:9, p. 157.
31. W-161.5:1–5, p. 304.
32. W-161.6:1, p. 304.

Chapter 4. The Separation
1. T-1.VI.1:6–8, p. 13.
2. T-3.VII.3:2–4:1, p. 50.
3. T-31.I.4:5, p. 646.
4. T-6.II.1:4–5, p. 96.
5. T-14.VII.4:3–7, pp. 287–88.
6. T-10.II.1:1–6, p. 183.
7. T-4.VI.1:6–7, p. 67.
8. T-Intro.1:7, p. 1.
9. T-12.III.7:1–10, p. 222.

Chapter 5. The World
1. T-16.V.3:6, p. 341.
2. W-132.5:1–2, p. 242.
3. T-12.IV.1:4, p. 223.
4. M-13.5:7–8, p. 34.
5. T-12.III.9:1, p. 222.
6. C-4.1:1–5, p. 85.
7. T-29.VI.2:7–10, p. 616.
8. William Shakespeare, *Hamlet*, act 2, scene 2, line 252.

9.   T-12.III.9:6–10, pp. 222–23.
10. T-5.V.4:1–3, p. 84.
11. T-21.in.1:2–8, p. 445.
12. T-21.V.1:1–2, 7, p. 456.
13. T-31.I.13:1–5, p. 648.
14. T-8.III.4:1–7, p. 142.
15. T-17.III.8:2, p. 357.
16. T-14.XI.3:1, p. 296.
17. M-24.6:3–7, p. 61.
18. T-1.VII.4:1, p. 16.

Chapter 6. The Real World

1.   T-30.V.1:1–2, p. 635.
2.   T-13.VII.9:1, p. 255.
3.   T-11.VII.1:1–3, p. 210.
4.   W-166.10:3–7, p. 316.
5.   C-in.2:5–6, p. 77.
6.   T-31.V.8:3–9:1, pp. 657–58.
7.   T-13.VII.2:1–3, p. 254.
8.   W-158.7:1–5, p. 299.
9.   W-159.3:1–3, p. 300.
10. T-13.V.9:1–4, p. 249.
11. W-37.1:2–3, p. 56.
12. T-29.III.3:12–13, p. 611.
13. W-134.7:1–3, p. 249.
14. W-181.8:3–6, p. 338.
15. W-271.1:3, p. 432.
16. W-pII.10.2:1–5:3, p. 455.
17. W-152.8:3–4, p. 282.
18.   M-14.5:1–8, p. 37.

19. T-11.VIII.1:8–9, p. 211.

20. W-188.1:4, p. 357.

21. T-17.II.4:4–5, p. 353.

22. T-11.VIII.1:5–7, p. 211.

23. T-27.III.6:7–7:9, p. 574.

Chapter 7. Decision

1. T-12.VII.9:1, p. 231.

2. T-17.III.9:1–8, p. 357.

3. T-5.V.6:6–14, p. 85.

4. T-1.I.1:1–3, p. 3.

5. W-138.4:1–8, p. 264.

6. T-29.IV.1:4–5, p. 612.

7. T-14.III.16:1–4, p. 278.

8. T-14.IV.5:1–4, p. 280.

9. T-9.V.9:6, p. 173; cf. Matthew 7:16, 20.

10. T-14.III.9:3–5, p. 276.

11. T-6.V-C.4:9–5:2, p. 110.

12. T-16.II.3:3, p. 352.

13. T-31.VI.1:1–8, p. 660.